Rev. & Mrs. Kyle McQuillen
1561 Avon Place
Huntington IN 46750

ANSWERING GOD

Also by Eugene H. Peterson

ANSWERING GOD

The Psalms as Tools for Prayer

Eugene H. Peterson

1817

Harper & Row, San Francisco

New York, Grand Rapids, Philadelphia, St. Louis
London, Singapore, Sydney, Tokyo, Toronto

For Jan, again

ANSWERING GOD. Copyright © 1989 by Eugene H. Peterson. All rights reserved. Printed in the United States of America. No part of this book may be used or reproduced in any manner whatsoever without written permission except in the case of brief quotations embodied in critical articles and reviews. For information address Harper & Row, Publishers, Inc., 10 East 53rd Street, New York, NY 10022.

Library of Congress Cataloging-in-Publication Data
Peterson, Eugene H.
   Answering God.

   Bibliography: p.
   1. Bible. O.T. Psalms—Devotional
use. 2. Prayer. I. Title.
BS1430.5.P47   1989   223'.2   88-45992
ISBN 0-06-066502-5

89   90   91   92   93   HC   10   9   8   7   6   5   4   3   2

Contents

Acknowledgments

I wrote much of this book in a home on the Flathead Lake in Montana while on a sabbatical year away from my congregation. My parents had lived in it until their deaths three years earlier. As a boy I carried boards and handed up tools to my father as he built the first version of it. For forty-five years it has been a place of renewal, retreat, and prayer for our family members: my parents, my sister and brother and their families, my family. As my wife and I lived in it by ourselves on this sabbatical year, the life of faith of my parents seemed very present and alive. I became aware of how much of their work and prayers had been absorbed into my life—my praying, working, and believing life. Many days as I wrote I felt like I was harvesting grain from their lives. What they had planted, I was reaping.

My Maryland congregation, Christ Our King Presbyterian Church, was involved in a different way—providing the sabbatical year, praying, and affirming. Few pastors, I think, have been as blessed in a congregation. Students at St. Mary's Seminary and Ecumenical Institute in Baltimore, Louisville Presbyterian Seminary, Fuller Seminary, and New College Berkeley through their questions and affirmations have deepened and matured the material.

Along the way friends gave direction, encouragement, and assistance: Russ and Cathie Reid, Ken Korby, Terry McGonigal, Constance FitzGerald, O.C.D., Steve Trotter, Jeffrey Wilson, Jim Riddell. Jan, my wife, listened as I read early drafts and tested them for honesty. Christine Anderson was inventive in many kindnesses as she managed the production of the book. Barbara Groves, generous in her help and skilled in her administration, typed the several drafts, cheerfully and (it seemed) effortlessly using her considerable competence in computer science to the glory of God.

Introduction

The human, in a classic definition, is the tool-making creature, *homo faber*. We are not animals, living by sheer instinct, in immediate touch with our environment. We are not angels, living by sheer intelligence, with unmediated access to God. We are creatures, heavily involved with tools. Unlike animals, we use knife and fork to get food to our mouths, and hammer and saw to build a home for ourselves. Unlike the angels, we use the scriptures to hear what God says to us, and the sacraments to receive his life among us.

The human, in another definition, is the creature that prays, *homo pecator*. The two definitions are the same. Prayer is technology. Prayers are tools.

Tools, though, are not the most important thing about us; God is: God in action creating, redeeming, and blessing. God makes the universe. God comes incarnate in Christ. God pours out his Spirit on creatures and creation.

And tools are not the most evident thing about us; we are: the way our bodies function and our minds work, making love and making a living, our feelings of goodness and awfulness, asking questions about our origins and ends, sometimes believing and sometimes doubting the answers that we receive.

But in the business of being human, even though neither most important or most evident, tools are required. Every distinctive human behavior requires tools: farming, loving, cooking, learning, building, believing. Some tools are made of wood, some of metal, some of words. A tool that is made of words is no less a tool than one made of steel. Prayer is a tool that is made, mostly, of words.

All the tools are essential: the plow for farming, the book for learning, pots for cooking, prayers for believing. All the sources of our action—body, mind, spirit—are dependent on tools. Every part of our humanity is in the tool-using business. Life is the issue, human life: living well, living whole in a world in which God is in action. To live as a human being means that we use tools. Animals get by without tools, and angels get by without tools, but humans need tools. We live well or badly by means of the tools we have and how well we use them.

Tools for Being and Becoming

Prayers are tools, but with this clarification: prayers are not tools for doing or getting, but for being and becoming. In our largely externalized culture, we are urgently presented with tools that enable us to *do* things (a machine, for instance, to clean the carpet), and to *get* things (a computer, for instance, to get information). We are also well trained in their use. We are not so readily offered tools that enable our being and becoming human. We are accustomed to think of our age as conspicuously technological. But the largest area of the human continent is impoverished technologically. The vaunted technologies of our day are used only along the shoreline of the human condition; the vast interiors are bereft. The consequence is that, lacking adequate tools (a technology), most people don't venture into these interiors, at least not very far. Life is constricted on the boundary, between ocean and wilderness, where a narrow competence in doing and getting is exercised.

At the center of the whole enterprise of being human, prayers are the primary technology. Prayers are tools that God uses to work his will in our bodies and souls. Prayers are tools that we use to collaborate in his work with us.[1]

For the tool-making, tool-using creatures who venture into the ocean depths of being and journey into the wilderness frontiers of becoming, making and being made into eternal habitations, the Psalms are the requisite toolbox. The Psalms are the best tools available for working the faith—one hundred and fifty carefully crafted prayers that deal with the great variety of operations that God carries on in us and attend to all the parts of our lives that are, at various times and in different ways, rebelling and trusting, hurting and praising. People of faith take possession of the Psalms with the same attitude and for the same reason that gardeners gather up rake and hoe on their way to the vegetable patch, and students carry paper and pencil as they enter a lecture hall. It is a simple matter of practicality—acquiring the tools for carrying out the human work at hand.

Two things are notable about the Psalms. One is that in the practice of prayer they have been marked by an extravagant claim. The other is that in the history of prayer they stand out with an awkward singularity.

An Extravagant Claim

The extravagant claim is that the Psalms are necessary. Is "necessary" too strong a word? They are not necessary to salvation— "by grace you have been saved through faith; and this is not your own doing, it is the gift of God—not because of works, lest anyone should boast" (Eph. 2:8-9). Our prayers, whether clumsy or skilled, heretical or orthodox, verbatim from the Psalter or ad libbed from a sinking ship, get us no merit with God. Nor are the Psalms necessary to validate our prayer as genuine—God hears anything we whisper or shout, say or sing. Right words and correct forms are not prerequisite to a heavenly audience. God is not fastidious in these matters.

All the same, they are necessary. The consensus on this, throughout the church's praying life, is impressive.[2] If we wish to develop in the life of faith, to mature in our humanity, and to glorify God with our entire heart, mind, soul, and strength, the Psalms are necessary. We cannot bypass the Psalms. They are God's gift to train us in prayer that is comprehensive (not patched together from emotional fragments scattered around that we chance upon) and honest (not a series of more or less sincere verbal poses that we think might please our Lord).[3]

The Psalms are necessary because they are the prayer masters. What is a master?

"Not one who one imitates, emulates even, but rather, a powerful presence acknowledged, looked up to in all weathers, A mountain. A great upheaval of rock and earth. Contours, declivities, the tufted ridge that defines the horizon, curly bloom of foggy woods, a rock face far up implying 'the sounding cataract'. . . . The mountain is master of the landscape in which it is a presence. One does not emulate such a master, except by being more oneself."[4]

We apprentice ourselves to these masters, acquiring facility in using the tools, by which we become more and more ourselves.

If we are willfully ignorant of the Psalms, we are not thereby excluded from praying, but we will have to hack our way through formidable country by trial and error and with inferior tools. If we dismiss the Psalms, preferring a more up-to-date and less demanding school of prayer, we will not be without grace, but we will miss the center where Christ worked in his praying. Christ prayed the Psalms—the Christian community was early convinced that he continues praying them through us as we pray them: "we recite this prayer of the Psalm in Him, and He recites it in us."[5]

An Awkward Singularity

The awkward singularity is that the Psalms do not "fit" into a form people naturally gravitate to in prayer. In the history of prayer, the Psalms are queer fish.

Most students of the human condition agree that prayer is basic to our existence. Prayer reaches into the unknown for whatever we sense, deep within us, will provide wholeness, or for what we hope, far off, will bring salvation. There is more to being human than simply surviving; there is God (or gods or "higher powers")—looking for God, pleasing God, getting God's help. We are unfinished creatures—longing, reaching, stretching towards fulfillment. We express these desires for completion in prayer. Prayers articulate our seeking after the best. Prayers give voice to aspiration towards the highest. Everything that is distinctively human gets formulated in prayers: our pathos, our nobility, our creativity. Also, interestingly, everything that is disreputable in us—lust, avarice, pride, pettiness—disguises itself in prayer in order, if possible, to get us credit instead of shame. But either way, whether in disguise or reality, prayers show us at our best.

Except for the Psalms. The Psalms set their faces against this lush eroticism, this rank jungle growth of desire seeking fulfillment. In a world of prayers that indulge the religious ego and cultivate passionate longings, the Psalms stand out with a kind of angular austerity. The Psalms are acts of obedience, answering the God who has addressed us. God's word precedes these words: these prayers don't seek God, they respond to the God who seeks us. These responses are often ones of surprise, for who expects God to come looking for us? And they are sometimes awkward, for in our religious striving we are usually looking for something quite other than the God who has come looking for us. God comes and speaks—his word catches us in sin, finds us in despair, invades us by grace. The Psalms are our answers. We don't always like what God speaks to us, and we don't always understand it. Left to ourselves, we will pray to some god who speaks what we like hearing, or to the part of God that we manage to understand. But what is critical is that we speak to the God who speaks to us, and to everything that he speaks to us, and in our speaking (which gathers up our listening and answering) mature in the great art of conversation with God that is prayer. The Psalms—all of which listen in order to answer—train us in the conversation.

The erotic (human pathos, nobility, and creativity seeking for what it does not have) is not absent from the Psalms. It would not be possible to have authentically human speech here without it; but it is not encouraged—it is wrestled into obedience, subjected to the strenuous realities of living by faith in the God who reveals himself to us. And that accounts for the odd and awkward singularity of the Psalms, for instead of being tributaries into the flow of the great prayer-river of longing for the Absolute, they abruptly stand us up, our lungs half-full of water, coughing and sputtering our unrehearsed answers to the God who calls us into a life of covenant, speaking salvation to us.

There is a difference between praying to an unknown God whom we hope to discover in our praying, and praying to a known God, revealed through Israel and in Jesus Christ, who speaks our language. In the first we indulge our appetite for religious fulfillment; in the second we practice obedient faith. The first is a lot more fun; the second is a lot more important. What is essential in prayer is not that we learn to express ourselves, but that we learn to answer God. The Psalms show us how to answer.

Redigging the Wells the Philistines Filled

It is not easy to understand how anything so deeply understood and widely practiced—the Psalms as the technology of prayer—should have shrunk in our time to a mere remnant. For some, who don't know their use, it is a matter of ignorance: in the shattering of traditions and consequent amnesia in our world, it often happens that we get cut off from our sources without ever being aware of it. For others, it is intimidation: in an age of experts, when we come across things that seem complex and that we don't immediately understand, it is easy to conclude that these matters can only be handled by professionals. And for some, I hope not most, it is simply sloth: it is easier to pray on whim and by impulse than to apprentice ourselves to a master, be forced to leave the ruts of mediocrity, and *climb*.

But whatever the reasons, something can be done. A recovery of the Psalms as the primary technology for developing a life of prayer is possible. In the face of the appalling adolescence of so much American spirituality, I think it is imperative. I want to do what I can to assist in the recovery. I am helpless before the sloth, but I can do something about ignorance and intimidation, and I write to that purpose: to recover the Psalms in their character as the tools of faith for those who don't know that is what they are for or who have been intimidated from ever picking them up, supposing that one needs a lot of training to be competent in their use.

My work, like Isaac digging again the wells that the Philistines had filled, is to clear the ground and cart off the debris so that what was so excellently done once will again be usable. There is nothing (I hope) innovative in what I write. This is not the latest thing on prayer, but the oldest: the Psalms, obvious and accessible as tools for prayer in the work of faith. So I do not explain them: commentary is not the primary need.[6] I want to provide a kind of owner's manual. I don't mean to suggest that the Psalms are easy: prayer is not easy. But the practice of millions of Christians through centuries of use is adequate proof that we do not have to acquire expertise in the Psalms before we use them; they themselves—prayers that train us in prayer—are the means to proficiency. We don't have to understand a crowbar before we put it to use. Understanding comes with use.

The practice of Christians in praying the Psalms is straightforward: simply pray through the Psalms, psalm by psalm, regularly. John Calvin expressed the consensus of the praying church when he wrote that the Psalms are "the design of the Holy Spirit . . . to deliver to the church a common form of prayer."[7] People who belong to liturgical traditions (Roman Catholic, Eastern Orthodox, Lutheran, Episcopal) have prayer books to guide them through a monthly cycle of praying the Psalms daily. The rest of us can easily mark the Psalms into thirty or sixty daily sections to guide an orderly monthly or bimonthly praying of all the Psalms. That's it: open our Bibles to the book of Psalms and pray them—sequentially, regularly, faithfully across a lifetime. This is how most Christians for most of the Christian centuries have matured in prayer. Nothing fancy. Just do it. The praying itself is deliberate and leisurely, letting (as St. Benedict directed) the motions of the heart come into harmony with the movements of the lips.[8]

I have laid up thy word in my heart
that I may not sin against thee.

PSALM 119:11

If you abide in me, and my words abide in you, ask whatever
you will and it shall be done for you.

JESUS (JOHN 15:7)

Everything depends on how we read, on how we enter the
magic circle of a text's meanings; on how we smuggle
ourselves into its words, and allow the texture of a text to
weave its web around us.

MICHAEL FISHBANE

1. Text

A text has texture. Words, woven into a fabric of meaning, have a characteristic *feel* to them. When our fingers touch textiles, we know what they are good for by their feel—silk for hair ribbons, denim for bib overalls, wool for a ski sweater. When our eyes go over the words of a text and our tongues and lips reproduce the sound of the words, we get a feel for how they are being used and how to take them. Getting the feel of the text is prerequisite to getting its meaning, for if we don't know how to *take* words, we will probably take them incorrectly. When we hear words spoken, we pick this up easily through tone and rhythm. Words spoken harshly and jerkily mean one thing, softly and languidly another, and in measured monotone still another—the dictionary meaning of the words is the same each time; the intended and received meaning different. When we read words that are written, we compensate for loss of voice by observing how the words are arranged in the loom of the text. As we discern the texture, we know how to take the text.

The Psalms are poetry and the Psalms are prayer: this is the texture of the text.

Poetry and Prayer

Poetry is language used with personal intensity. It is not, as so many suppose, decorative speech. Poets tell us what our eyes, blurred with too much gawking, and our ears, dulled with too much chatter, miss around and within us. Poets use words to drag us into the depth of reality itself. They do it not by reporting on how life is, but by pushing-pulling us into the middle of it. Poetry grabs for the jugular. Far from being cosmetic language, it is intestinal. It is root language. Poetry doesn't so much tell us something we never knew as bring into recognition what is latent, forgotten, overlooked, or suppressed.[1] The Psalms text is almost entirely in this kind of language. Knowing this, we will not be looking here primarily for ideas about God, or for direction in moral conduct. We will expect, rather, to find the experience of being human before God exposed and sharpened.

Prayer is language used in personal relation to God. It gives utterance to what we sense or want or respond to before God. God speaks to us; our answers are our prayers. The answers are not always articulate: silence, sighs, groaning—these also constitute responses. The answers are not always positive: anger, skepticism, curses—these also are responses. But always God is involved, whether in darkness or light, whether in faith or despair. This is hard to get used to. Our habit is to talk about God, not to him. We love discussing God. The Psalms resist these discussions. They are not provided to teach us about God but to train us in responding to him. We don't learn the Psalms until we are praying them.

This texture, the poetry and the prayer, accounts for both the excitement and difficulty in dealing with this text. The poetry requires that we deal with our actual humanity—these words dive beneath the surfaces of prose and pretense, straight into the depths. We are more comfortable with prose, the laid-back language of our arms-length discourse. The prayer requires that we deal with God—this God who is determined on nothing less than the total renovation of our lives. We would rather have a religious bull session.

Soil and Weather

Specific conditions account for the particular texture of the Psalms. These conditions do not assertively call attention to themselves. Conditions never do. They—the climate, terrain, and culture we grow up in that determine much of who we are and become, but that we are so used to that we don't notice—are just quietly there. So it is possible to have an extensive informational acquaintance with the Psalms without being aware of the conditions determinative of their being. The astonishing bloom and blossom blazing in the Psalms cannot be cultivated into maturity in us apart from entering into, insofar as we are able, the soil and weather conditions in which they came to flower. It is impossible for the Psalms to become prayer in us unless we embrace the conditions in which they were prayed. We cannot abstract the Psalms from their conditions. We cannot substitute conditions congenial to our temperament. Since the Psalms are the classic texts that train us in prayer, it is essential that we immerse ourselves in their "soil and weather." Our purpose is to grow a garden, not just cut a few flowers. Three conditions are definitive: a revealed theology, a defined canon, and a practiced liturgy.

Theology: The One God

God (*theos*) is the single most important condition accounting for the Psalms. The God without which the Psalms could not exist is the God who reveals himself in Israel and in Christ. He makes himself known. Because he makes himself known, he is a God whom we know. It is required, therefore, that we use our minds to think on him, not lazily (or anxiously) guess our way. Hence theology: people of faith using their minds to understand who God is and how he works.

In an age and among a people saturated with psychology, it is hard to concede primacy to theology in anything, not exempting religious texts. With the Psalms, brimming with human experience and explosive with energies of soul (*psyche*)—John Calvin called them "an anatomy of all the parts of the soul"—it is virtually impossible not to work on the assumption that psychology has the primacy. We want to understand these souls in their intimacy and depth, these souls that quail at nothing, push through frontiers in their exploration of meaning, vigorously grappling with everything they encounter across the entire spectrum of experience. Here is the deeply felt, honestly voiced raw data of the human condition—an open invitation, it would seem, for the curious and disciplined intelligence to conduct a searching examination. And who is better prepared to carry out that examination than a psychologically trained people?

And besides, isn't prayer mostly psychology anyway? We are complex persons, full of unconscious yearnings and unnamed desires, vast interiors that call out for enlightenment and understanding. Every prayer in one way or another, reveals something of these interiors. Who can resist the offer of psychology to put these prayers out on the table alongside our dreams, phobias, and test scores for study and analysis? How much we will understand about ourselves when we have finished!

But the Psalms were not prayed by people trying to understand themselves. They are not the record of people searching for the meaning of life. They were prayed by people who understood that God had everything to do with them. God, not their feelings, was the center. God, not their souls, was the issue. God, not the meaning of life, was critical. Feelings, souls, and meanings were not excluded—they are very much in evidence—but they are not the reason for the prayers. Human experiences might provoke the prayers, but they do not condition them *as* prayers.

If we come to the Psalms looking for a way to develop our inner life, we have come to the wrong place. Kahlil Gibran is a better bet. If we come to the Psalms in search for peak experiences, we have made a wrong choice. The psalmists are not interested in human potential; they are passionate about *God*—the obedience-shaping, will-transforming, sin-revoking, praise-releasing God.

The Psalms come from a people who hear God speak to them and realize that it is the most important word they will ever hear spoken. They decide to respond. They answer. The word they hear from God takes precedence over every human word: human wisdom, human advice, human discourse, human inquiry. These people made their mark in history not by understanding themselves or studying what they found around them in earth and sky, but in praying to the God who revealed himself to them in Word. All around them their Greek, Assyrian, Babylonian, and Egyptian neighbors gave themselves in intelligent passion to exploring the surface of the earth, plotting the stars and tracking the constellations, mastering the uses of power, pursuing questions of truth, figuring out how numbers worked. The results of all this physical and mental activity are breathtakingly magnificent. The Hebrews prayed. They were intelligent and passionate before God. They knew that God had invaded their history. They knew themselves addressed by God. They responded to the presence; they answered the address; they prayed.

It is not simply belief in a supreme being that conditions these prayers, belief in a divinity that they must deal with in order to make their way through life, avoiding, if possible, disaster, and promoting, hopefully, good fortune. The determinative condition is a God who speaks and acts in a known way. The condition is not a *belief* in God, but a *doctrine* of God.

It is not possible to comprehend God. Merely to utter the name "God" is to be plunged into mystery. But that doesn't mean that we are in the dark, where all cats are gray. At least it did not for the Hebrews, or the praying Christians in their train. None of them knew very much about God, but they knew a few things with clarity. They did not wistfully wish upwards,[3] they had a *doctrine* of God. Some things were true: Adamic creation, Abrahamic covenant, Exodus salvation, Mosaic commands. Some things were not true: God was not arbitrary, not destructive, not indifferent, not manipulable.

They took the trouble to find out what was revealed, to observe closely, to understand responsibly, to use their heads, and then to respond, to answer. History was usually a puzzle. Their own souls were mostly murky. But they went to their knees in a pool of light—an illuminating word, two words, maybe even a few sentences that revealed God to them, and by which they courageously decided to live in faith. The Psalms are personal answers to the personal revelation, prayers conditioned by God's word, not by the soul's moods.

Canon: The Sixty-six Books

The Psalms come to us embedded in Holy Scripture. They have their own identity as a book, 150 prayers with a clearly marked beginning and end. They are, at the same time, an integral part of a larger book, the Bible. The only way we know the Psalms is in this context. They do not arrive independently. They do not present themselves to us in their own right. The Psalms are not scraps of prayer, found in bottles on beaches from time to time, arrived from an unknown country. We know that country very well and quite a lot about the people who prayed and wrote the prayers. We know what they experienced and what they hoped for. We know the battles they fought, the marriages they contracted, the children they reared, the cities they lived in, the mountains they climbed, the rivers they crossed, and the wells they drank from. We know what their priests wore in making sacrifice for their sins. We know what their prophets preached to them. We know their names and the names of their enemies. These psalms are not like Melchizedek—"without father or mother or genealogy." They have the Torah for their mother, the Prophets for their father, and a luxuriantly rambling family tree.

The canon (the two testaments of sixty-six books that are authoritative for the Christian faith) is a corral, fencing in all the literary creatures conceived and born out of a common inspiration and that serve a common purpose. (The common inspiration is the Holy Spirit; the common purpose salvation.) Many of these creatures bear little or no resemblance to each other. Some of them we don't like at all. Others we become fond of and develop close friendships. But the canonical decision was that our preferences are not determinative in these matters: all the creatures are related in some way or other to all the others, and each in its own way serves the common purpose. Each is necessary, but none is complete in itself. Each must be used (interpreted) in the light of all the others. It is not permitted to take one of the creatures out of the corral, leaving all others behind, and ride out across the prairies sentimentally into the sunset, searching for conditions congenial to sublimity. There is no gate in the corral fence.

This means that the Psalms are part *of* something before they are anything—part of Genesis, Joshua, and Esther; part of Matthew, Romans, and the Apocalypse. Since the Psalms are not themselves by themselves, they cannot be prayed in isolation from their context, those sixty-five other "creatures" that God uses to shape salvation in us.

When we learn to speak, we have ancestral genes doing their work in us and are surrounded by family traditions, heirlooms, social expectations, and cultural assumptions. We use words others used before us, each word carrying the experience of generations. If we expressed ourselves uniquely (as we sometimes do in our first few months), no one would understand us.

The Psalms likewise are infused with and surrounded by a genetic, cultural, worshiping, and believing heritage. This canonical condition means that in the life of faith we don't make up original prayers that suit our private spiritual genius. Prayer is not an original language, but a received language.

A millennium's experience of grace and judgment, creation and chaos, guilt and salvation, rebellion and obedience shapes the prayers that are the Psalms. When we pray the Psalms, and are trained in prayer by them, we enter into this centuries-long experience of being a people of God. We didn't bargain on this: we wanted a little book of prayers that we could keep on our bedside table, not the genealogies in Chronicles, for heaven's sake. But it can't be helped. If we want to associate with these people who pray and submit our lives to this training in prayer, we are going to have to associate with their large, somewhat noisy and often troublesome family, for it is quite certain that the psalmists will not abandon their canonical company to tutor us to soliloquies customized to our genius.

Liturgy: The Two or Three Together

The praying people, whose prayers are the Psalms, prayed as a worshiping community. All the psalms are prayers in community: people assembled, attentive before God, participating in a common posture, movement and speech, offering themselves and each other to their Lord. Prayer is not a private exercise, but a family convocation.

In the presence of God, "alone" is not good. Summon Eve. Call a friend. "Where two or three are gathered together in my name, there I am in the midst of them." By ourselves, we are not ourselves. Solitary confinement is extreme punishment; private prayer is extreme selfishness. Prayer, in itself, is not an automatic good. It is possible to practice prayer in such a way that it drives us deep into a conniving, calculating egotism. And it is possible to practice prayer in such a way that it bloats us into a prideful ostentation. Jesus was not indiscriminate in his praise of prayer; some people who prayed got a severe tongue-lashing from him.

Prayer often originates when we are alone. Deep within us are "sighs too deep for words." We pray our guilt, our hurt, our gaiety on the spot, not waiting until we can meet with a congregation or get into a church. All the same, for these prayers to develop into full maturity, they must be integrated into the praying community.

And prayer continues into places of solitude. We pray on our beds at night, silently and secretly when surrounded by unbelievers, deliberately withdrawn from society in order to cleanse the "doors of perception."[4] We neither can or should be with others continuously; and we are with God continuously.

But the believing community at worship, at regular times and in assigned places, is the *base* of prayer. All the psalms were prayed in such communities. This is not obvious on the surface—we are apt to think of a shepherd on a grassy slope, or a traveler on a dangerous road—nevertheless, it is one of the assured results of devout research, confirmed in the practice of Israel and church. We are most congruent with the conditions in which the Psalms were produced and prayed when we pray in a praying congregation.

Sometimes a group diminishes us: we are leveled down, lumped into the less-than-average, and become less than ourselves. This happens when we are with people who gossip, or competitively assert themselves by cutting down others. This happens when we sink as a spectator into a crowd.

Other times we are exhilarated, lifted up, infused with energy and purpose, and become more than we are on our own. This happens when we share complementary effort and skills to play a game, climb a mountain, or run a successful business. This happens when we are with family members who accept one another with grace, mourn a common loss, celebrate a common joy. This happens when we pray in a worshiping congregation.

We are not naturally good at this. We need practice. Especially in the initial stages we feel uneasy, awkward, and bored. But it is God's will that we live by the lively exchanges of grace and in the splendid movements of love, and neither grace nor love are possible without friends and enemies. Prayer is the primary means by which we develop our lives in these communities before God, and the Psalms train us in it.

The Psalms train us to pray with others who have prayed, and are praying: put our knees on the level with other bent knees; lift our hands in concert with other lifted hands; join our voices in lament and praise with other voices who weep and laugh. The primary use of prayer is not for expressing ourselves, but in becoming ourselves, and we cannot do that alone. The "only child" is not God's. It follows that this primary condition in the making of the Psalms, praying "in step" with others, is also a condition for praying them and learning to pray.

Against the Grain

Not one of these conditions is congenial to the way most of us would prefer to go at the business of praying. They go against the religious grain, and especially against the American grain. We would rather pray by exploring our own deep spiritual capacities, with God as background music. We would rather pray by meditating on some sublime truth, without bothering with the tedium and complexity of the scriptures. We would rather pray by having God all to ourselves, insulated from the irritating presence of other people, and savor (but only a little) a smug sense of superiority to the common herd. But the text that teaches us to pray comes with conditions, and the conditions won't permit us to isolate ourselves. If we elect the Psalms to train us in prayer, these are the conditions in which we will be working.

The Lord knows the way of the righteous,
but the way of the wicked will perish.

PSALM 1:6

The way is hard that leads to life, and those who find it are
few.

JESUS (MATTHEW 7:14)

To arrive where you are, to get from where you are not, You
must go by a way wherein there is no ecstasy.

T. S. ELIOT

2. Way

The text that teaches us to pray doesn't begin with prayer. We are not ready. We are wrapped up in ourselves. We are knocked around by the world. The ways in which we are used to going about our business, using the language, dealing with our neighbors, and thinking about God don't exactly disqualify us from prayer, but neither do they help much.

The nonpraying world is a pushing, shoving, demanding world. Voices within and without harass, insisting that we look at this picture, read this headline, listen to this appeal, feel this guilt, touch this charm. It is asking too much that we move from this high-stimulus world into the quiet concentrations of prayer without an adequate transition.

The nonpraying world is also an intimidating world. We wake each day to a world noisy with braggadocio, violent with guns, arrogant with money. What use is prayer in the face of governments, armies, and millionaires? What motivation can we muster to pray when all the obvious power is already allocated to heads of state and barons of industry?

In prayer we intend to leave the world of anxieties and enter a world of wonder. We decide to leave an ego-centered world and enter a God-centered world. We will to leave a world of problems and enter a world of mystery. But it is not easy. We are used to anxieties, egos, and problems; we are not used to wonder, God, and mystery.

Pre-Prayer

Psalms 1 and 2 pave the way. They get us ready to pray. The Psalms are an edited book. All these prayers were collected and arranged at one point in Israel's history, and then Psalms 1 and 2 set as an entrance to them, pillars flanking the way into prayer. We are not unceremoniously dumped into the world of prayer, we are courteously led across an ample porch, a way that provides space and means by which we are adjusted to the realities of prayer. *Way* is a significant word in the first two Psalms.

Psalms 1 and 2 are a pair, working together to put our feet on the path that goes from the nonpraying world in which we are habitually distracted and intimidated, into the praying world where we come to attention and practice adoration. For prayer is not only a matter of saying the right sort of words to the right kind of God. Our *being* is involved, the *way* we are.

Psalms 1 and 2 are pre-prayer, getting us ready, making us adequate for prayer. We never get past needing this help. We hunger and thirst for God, but our noblest appetites are debased by our own fears and lusts and the stamp the culture presses upon us. Unless we have help out of ourselves, our prayers will only be verbal and emotional projections from our nonpraying world. "Knowing demands the organ fitted to the object."[1] We have well-developed organs fit for finding a bargain, driving Subarus, and reading *Huckleberry Finn*; our "organs" for knowing God are not so well exercised. Preparation of the pray-er, necessarily precedes the act of praying. The old wisdom in this matter is: "Whatever is received is received according to the mode of the one receiving it."[2] Psalms 1 and 2 put us in the way (mode) of prayer. Psalm 1 is the way from intimidation to adoration.

The first word of the first psalm, *blessed,* sets the tone: happy, fortunate, lucky with holy luck. The second psalm uses the same word at its finish. Jesus took this *blessed* ("seized" is more like it), used it as the first word in his most famous sermon, and then elaborated it into an octave, an eight-line stanza (Matthew 5:3–10).

Blessed is a directional antenna, a mind-set for picking up signals we would otherwise miss. We get ready to pray. What are we getting into? We are on the outskirts of his ways, about to enter the deep interiors. What is the appropriate attitude before this unknown? Apprehension will make us cautious, crippled for taking risks, if risks need to be taken. Stoic dutifulness will make us heavy-footed, clumsy in the dance, if a dance is scheduled. The *blessed* arouses expectation, a readiness for a more that is also a good. We don't know the contents of the *blessed*, or the difficulties—how could we, we are not there yet?—but we sense that we are entering a way on which we will become more our true selves, not less, not other. The anticipation of being blessed works changes in us that make us capable of being blessed.

Coming to Attention: Psalm 1

Two things are prominent in Psalm 1: an action and an image. Torah-meditation is the action; a transplanted tree is the image.

Torah (law) is God's words that hit the target of the human condition. The noun *torah* comes from a verb, *yarah*, that means to throw something, a javelin, say, so that it hits its mark. The word that hits its mark is *torah*. In living speech, words are javelins hurled from one mind into another. The javelin word goes out of one person and pierces another. Not all words are javelins; some are only tin cans, carrying information from one place to another. But God's word has this aimed, intentional, personal nature. When we are spoken to this way, piercingly and penetratingly, we are not the same. These words get inside us and work their meaning in us.[3]

As we prepare to pray, to answer the words God addresses to us, we learn that all of God's words have this characteristic: they are *torah* and we are the target. God's word is not a reference book in a library that we pull off the shelf when we want information. There is nothing inert or bookish in these words. God's words, creating and saving words every one, hit us where we live.

The moment we know this, that God speaks to us, delight is spontaneous. "The psalms are the liturgy for those whose concern and delight is the torah of the Lord".[4] These are not words that we laboriously but impersonally study, as if for an exam.

These are not words that we anxiously scan lest we inadvertently transgress a boundary or break a protocol. These are words we *take* in—words designed for shaping new life in us, feeding the energies of salvation. This delight develops into meditation, torah-meditation. Meditate *(hagah)* is a bodily action; it involves murmuring and mumbling words, taking a kind of physical pleasure in making the sounds of the words, getting the *feel* of the meaning as the syllables are shaped by larynx and tongue and lips.[5] Isaiah used this word "meditate" for the sounds that a lion makes over its prey (Isa. 31:4). A lion over its catch and a person over the torah act similarly. They purr and growl in pleasurable anticipation of taking in what will make them more themselves, strong, lithe, swift: "I will run in the way of thy commandments when thou enlargest my understanding!" (Ps. 119:32).

This is quite different from merely reading God's word, or thinking about it. This is not so much an intellectual process, figuring out meanings, as it is a physical process, hearing and rehearing these words as we sound them again, letting the sounds sink into our muscles and bones. Meditation is mastication.

A transplanted tree provides the image that locates us in the way of prayer.[6] Letting the psalm words carry their most natural meaning, "a tree planted by streams of water " is "a tree transplanted alongside irrigation canals." Israel, during the time that the psalms were collected and made into its prayer book, was in Babylonian exile. Babylon was flat and featureless. A single river flowed through the country. The Babylonians had cut a network of irrigation canals across the land, multiplying the square miles of fertility. Transplanted to the banks of these irrigation ditches the Israelites—refugees under a merciless sun—thought they were in the worst possible place for prayer. Solomon's splendid temple was a pile of ruins back in Jerusalem. They didn't think they could pray. One of them composed a song, a kind of "Babylonian blues" that soon everyone was singing: "How can we sing the Lord's song in a strange land?" (Psalm

137). They didn't think they could. But they did. My, how they did it! How did they do it? By letting God's word enter their lives again, there in exile, and letting his address pull answers out of them. They immersed themselves in torah-meditation: before they knew it they were praying. They were trees. Transplanted to Babylon they put down roots, put out leaves, and produced fruit. We all suppose that we could pray, or pray better, if we were in the right place. We put off praying until we are where we think we should be, or want to be. We let our fantasies or our circumstances distract us from attending to the word of God that is aimed right where we are, and invites our answers from that spot.

We get ourselves ready to pray by looking at a tree, a transplanted tree, and seeing ourselves in it. "Before we can get to the great idea of True, an emotionally charged symbolic construct for which innumerable women and men have died, we must stare thoughtfully and long at a tree, Old English *Treow*, which gives us the word true *(Treow)*, the 'deeply rooted idea.' " [7]

Comprehension of the invisible begins in the visible. Praying to God begins by looking at a tree. The deepest relationship of which we are capable has its origin in the everyday experience of taking a good look at what is in everybody's backyard. We are not launched into the life of prayer by making ourselves more heavenly, but by immersing ourselves in the earthy: not by formulating abstractions such as goodness, beauty, or even God, but by attending to trees and tree toads, mountains and mosquitoes.

We come to the prayer book of the Bible to get training in prayer and the first directive is: "Go find yourself a tree, sit down in front of it, look at it long and thoughtfully." Prayer begins not with what we don't see, but with what we do see. Prayer begins in the senses, in the body, in geography, in botany.

Abstraction is an enemy to prayer. Beautiful ideas are an enemy to prayer. Fine thoughts are an enemy to prayer. Authentic prayer begins when we stub our toes on a rock, get drenched in a rainstorm, get slapped in the face by an enemy—or run into the tree that has been in our path for so long that we have ceased to see it, and now stand back, in bruised and wondering awe before it.

Torah-meditation is the action that moves us away from distracting words that push us this way and that; these words pull us into attentiveness. The transplanted tree is the image that focuses our distracted will, the will that is ever restlessly looking for and trying out the "right" conditions for prayer. The tree claims our attention and says, "Put your roots down *here.*"

Entering into Adoration: Psalm 2

The verb that dominates the action of Psalm 1, meditate *(ha-gah)*, is picked up in Psalm 2, but used in a context that requires the translation, "plot." "Why do the nations conspire, and the peoples *plot* in vain?" "Meditate" in Psalm 1 and "plot" in Psalm 2 are the same verb. And it is the same action: a murmuring, absorbed, ruminative interest over the word of God, realizing that this is *the* important word, the word that determines all existence. But while Psalm 1 directs us to approach this word with delight, receiving it as life-giving, Psalm 2 shows people plotting against this word, devising schemes for getting rid of it so that they can be free of all God-interference in their lives. These people see God's words not as javelins penetrating their lives with truth, but as chains that restrict their freedom. They put their minds together to rid themselves of this word so that their words can rule.

The people who do this appear impressive: they are both numerous (nations and peoples) and prominent (kings and rulers). A lot of people reject the word of God; they not only reject it, they turn their rejection into a world power. These people command most of the armies of the world, direct the advances of science, run school systems, preside over governments, and rule in the marketplaces. If these people are in active conspiracy against the rule of God, what difference can prayer make? What chance does mere "tree" meditating, have when the movers and shakers of the earth are conspiratorially aligned against it?

Intimidation is as fatal to prayer as distraction. If we are intimidated, we will forfeit the entire world of culture and politics, of business and science to those "who set themselves. . . . against the Lord."

What is at issue here is size: we require an act of imagination that enables us to see that the world of God is *large*—far larger than the worlds of kings and princes, prime ministers and presidents, far larger than the worlds reported by newspaper and television, far larger than the world described in big books by nuclear physicists and military historians. We need a way to imagine—to *see*—that the world of God's ruling word is not an afterthought to the worlds of the stock exchange, the rocket launching, and summit diplomacy, but itself contains them.

Far more is involved here than simply asserting God's sovereignty. We need a way, a convincing, usable, accessible tool for realizing the largeness of God in the midst of the competing bigness of the world. If we fail here, prayer will be stunted; we will pray huddled and cowering. Our prayers will whimper.

Psalm 2 answers our need by presenting Messiah. Messiah is God's person in history. God is not exclusively in the business of dealing with souls, he is also active in cities. Messiah is God's invasion of the secular, his entry into the world where people go to school, go to work, go to war, go to Chicago. He enters—and he enters *in person*. His word is not only what we meditate in the scriptures, it takes shape in history and we see it in action in a person.

This strikes many as implausible, that God, in order to develop within us a sense of the immensity of his rule, presents us with a human being with an ordinary name (Saul, David, Zerubbabel), in an unpretentious place (Zion), calls him "my son," and gives him unspiritual jobs like building roads, protecting cities, and dealing with foreign emissaries.

Objections are immediate and outraged: "But we grew up with him; we know his brothers and sisters; we sat across the aisle from him in the second grade and played ball with him in

Little League. Wouldn't it be better to put the brash world in its place by promulgating huge resolutions, by practicing large thoughts—truth, love, justice—and by sheer force of thinking overwhelm the vulgarity of the rulers? Or, if something visible is required, give directions for a statue that will humble the Sphinx, or provide blueprints for a temple that will fill a prairie?"

But nothing like that was done in Israel. Instead, people were selected and marked by pouring a flask of oil on their heads as representatives of God's rule, and so made messiahs (anointed ones). Israel was surrounded by world powers that boasted impressive temples, ruthless armies, Brobdingnagian statues, and extensive libraries. But when God wanted to show them how his rule was greater than anything that they saw around them, he directed that men be taken from local families and anointed. He trained them to look at the ordinary and the personal as the places where he initiated his rule and established his sovereignty. The people were turned away from trembling in awe or fear before the world's so-called mighty, they were patiently taught to see God working in and through messiah, an anointed one.

The extraordinary thing about this implausible method is that it works, at least for those who enter the way of prayer. Centuries of training in observing God's invasion of the world by messiah reached a conclusion when Jesus of Nazareth was declared Messiah (in Greek, *Christos*, "anointed one"). This Messiah was as implausible as the rest: "Is not this the son of Joseph?" (John 1:46). "Can any good come out of Nazareth?" (John 6:42). But it was true: God invaded history. In Jesus, Christians believe, the entrance was not only into history but into flesh, and the presence of God was not only representative but thoroughgoing. Jesus was the complete Messiah of which the earlier messiahs had been approximations. But the *method* was the same: God entered history in a human person and exercised his rule from that unassuming position in that unadorned person.

Two details encourage the expansion of the messianic imagination into adequacy. One shows God laughing at the world's rulers: "He who sits in the heavens laughs; the Lord has them in derision" (Psalm 2:4). Laughter restores perspective. There is such a thing as taking the world's arrogance too seriously. God laughs. We join him. In the laughter, every high-flown pretension is seen as silly posturing.

The other detail is a call to adoration: "Serve the Lord with fear, with trembling kiss his feet (Psalm 2:11)". We see the rulers needing a ruler, the kings needing a king. Their world is too small, the kingdoms over which they rule, trying to exclude God, too small. Their world is also dangerous. If they persist, they will be destroyed: "Therefore, O Kings, be wise: be warned" (Psalm 2:10). The trembling that reduces them to size opens them up to God's size. They need a larger world. The way to the larger world is through adoring reverence before the one who is more than they are.

This is not a sovereignty *imposed* on history or humans; it *invades*. It begins on the inside, not the outside. Those who embrace this way discover in the life of prayer that follows that the "inside is bigger than the outside."[8]

There is much yet to learn about how this Messiah works, and many misunderstandings to be worked through, but that is not the business of Psalm 2. That will come in its time in the practice of prayer and maturing in the faith. The work of Psalm 2 is to provide access to largeness, and thereby to rehabilitate the intimidated imagination so that it can grasp the enormous range of the word of God.

The Tree and the Messiah

The Hebrews arranged the scriptures into three sections: *Torah* (law) is the primary word of God; *Prophets* (including the historical books) shows God's word at work in geography and history; *Writings* (led by the Psalms) shape our response to God's word through the practice of prayer in the life of faith. God's word is surging and rich. Hundreds of years of words are in it— told in stories, preached in sermons, preserved in genealogies, interpreted in histories. Every syllable is a gem. Somehow or other, all those sharp, quick, and personal words must be heard and answered. Not a nuance must be lost. Psalms 1 and 2 work as funnels, directing all the *Torah* (through Psalm 1) and all the *Prophets* (through Psalm 2) into the way of prayer, that is, into the Psalms, where we take our place to get our lives trained by prayer "into an adequate answer to God's word."[9]

Psalm 1 is quiet, gathering our distracted lives into an act of supreme attention. Psalm 2 is vigorous, countering the bullying world that intimidates us into hiding. By means of Psalm 1 we become a tree, putting down roots into the soil and streams of Torah, collected and recollected before God's word. By means of Psalm 2 we observe Messiah, God personally involved in this world, often incognito, but *here*, and ruling. Psalm 1 concentrates our energies into listening attention. Psalm 2 expands our vision to take in the messianic revelation. At attention and in adoration, we are ready to pray.

Thou whose glory above the heavens is chanted
by the mouth of babes and infants,
thou hast founded a bulwark because of thy foes,
to still the enemy and the avenger.

PSALM 8:1–2

I thank thee, Father, Lord of heaven and earth, that thou hast
hidden these things from the wise and understanding and
revealed them to babes; yea, Father, for such was thy gracious
will. All things have been delivered to me by my Father, and
no one knows the Son except the Father, and no one knows
the Father except the Son and any one to whom the Son
chooses to reveal him.

JESUS (MATTHEW 11:25–27)

Language is not speech, it is a full circle from word to sound to
perception to understanding to feeling, to memorizing, to
acting and back to the word about the act thus achieved. And
before the listener can become a listener, something has to
happen to him: He must expect.

EUGEN ROSENSTOCK-HUESSY

3. Language

We prepare to pray not by composing our prayers but ourselves. The pre-prayers of Psalms 1 and 2 get us ready, forming the inner life so that it is adequate (the Thomist *adequatio*) to the reception of truth, not just the acquisition of facts.[1] But when we engage in the act of prayer itself, there is no preparing, no getting the right words, no posture to take, no mood to assume. We simply do it. Prayer is primal speech. We do not first learn how to do it, and then proceed to do it; we do it, in the doing we find out what we are doing, and then deepen and mature in it.

"O Lord, how many are my foes!" is thus the first sentence in the first prayer in the Psalms (3:1). Brief, urgent, frightened words—a person in trouble, crying out to God for help. The language is personal, direct, desperate. This is the language of prayer: men and women calling out their trouble—pain, guilt, doubt, despair—to God. Their lives are threatened. If they don't get help they will be dead, or diminished to some critical degree. The language of prayer is forged in the crucible of trouble. When we can't help ourselves and call for help, when we don't like where we are and want out, when we don't like who we are and want a change, we use primal language, and this language becomes the root language of prayer.

Language gets its start under the pressure of pain. Our first sound is a wail. All our early speech is an inarticulate eloquence that gets us what we need to survive: food, warmth, comfort, love. We need help. We need another. We are not furnished, as the lower animals are, with instincts that get us through the life cycle with minimal help from others. We are unfinished creatures requiring complex and extensive assistance in every part of our being, and language is the means for getting it.

Prayer, a human being conversing with a holy God, is a great mystery and defies probabilities. But it is a mystery embedded in something common and very close to us. In our learning to pray, God has not left us without a witness. Language itself, the way we learn it and the way we use it, is the witness. Human prayer arises out of the same conditions as human language. Prayer and language are not the same thing (we do not learn to pray simply by directing our language to God instead of parents and friends), but there are rich analogies between these two basic human practices. The nature of language provides insights into the learning and practice of prayer.

Mere Puffs of Wind

So observing the way language works is a good place to enter into the practice of prayer. Language is almost as much a mystery as prayer. There is irony here: our primary tool for understanding is not itself understood. After centuries of investigation, the people who study and ponder the way we learn and use words continue to spend much of their time astonished. "It remains wonderful that mere puffs of wind should allow men to discover what they think and feel, to share their attitudes and plans, to anticipate the future and learn from the past, and to create lasting works of art."[3]

Language is used at many different levels and for many different purposes. The language of prayer occurs primarily at one level, the personal, and for one purpose, salvation. The human condition teeters on the edge of disaster. Human beings are in trouble most of the time. Those who don't know they are in trouble are in the worst trouble. Prayer is the language of the people who are in trouble and know it, and who believe or hope that God can get them out. As prayer is practiced, it moves into other levels and develops other forms, but trouble—being in the wrong, being in danger, realizing that the foes are too many for us to handle—is the basic provocation for prayer. Isaac Bashevis Singer once said, "I only pray when I am in trouble. But I am in trouble all the time, and so I pray all the time." The recipe for obeying St. Paul's "Pray without ceasing" is not a strict ascetical regimen but a watchful recognition of the trouble we are in.

A rough map of the terrain that language inhabits is useful for locating the characteristics of prayer language. A division into three areas—Language I, Language II, and Language III—provides orientation.[3] These three broad divisions don't take account of the staggering complexities of language; in fact, they obscure them. But what we want from a map is help in getting someplace, not description and analysis of the soil. That can come later after we find out where we are.

Language Map

Language I is the language of personal intimacy and relationship. It is the first language we learn. At first it is not articulate speech. The sounds that pass between parent and infant are incredibly rich in meaning, but less than impressive in content. The coos and cries of the infant do not parse. The nonsense syllables of the answering parent have no dictionary entries. But in the exchange of gurgles and out-of-tune hums, trust develops. Parent whispers transmute infant screams into grunts of hope. The cornerstone words in this language are names, or pet names: mama, papa. For all its limited vocabulary and butchered syntax, it is more than adequate to express complex and profound love, and to develop the basic trust foundational to human existence. Language I is our primary language, the language we use to express and develop our human condition.

Language II is the language of information. As we grow we find a marvelous world of things surrounding us, and that everything has a name: rock, water, doll, bottle, finger. Gradually, through the acquisition of language, we are oriented in a world of objects. Beyond the relational intimacy with persons with which we begin, we find our way in an environment of trees and fire engines and snowballs. Day after day words are added. Things named are no longer strange. We explore the neighborhood. We make friends with the world. We learn to speak in sentences, making connections between this and that, between yesterday and tomorrow, between here and there. The world is wonderfully various, and our language enables us to account for it, to recognize what is here and how it is put together. Language II is the major language used in the schools.

Language III is the language of motivation. We discover early on that words have the power to make things happen, to bring something out of nothing, to move inert figures into purposive action. An infant brawl brings food and a dry diaper. A parental command arrests a childish tantrum. No physical force is involved. No material causation is visible. Just a word: stop, go, shut up, speak up, eat everything on your plate. We are moved by language and use it to move others. Children rapidly acquire proficiency in this language, moving people bigger and more intelligent than themselves to strenuous activity (often against both the inclination and better judgment of the people). Language III is the predominant language of advertising and politics.

Languages II and III are the ascendant languages of our culture. Language that describes (II) and language that motivates (III) dominate. We are well schooled in language that describes the world in which we live. We are well trained in the language that moves people to buy and join and vote. Meanwhile Language I, the language of intimacy, the language that develops relationships of trust, hope, and understanding, languishes. Once we are clear of the cradle we find less and less encouragement to use it. There is a short-lived recovery of Language I in adolescence when we fall in love and spend endless hours talking on the telephone using words that eavesdroppers characterize as gibberish. But it is the farthest thing from gibberish: the sounds express relationship, they are a realization of *being*. These young people are listening to the sounds of being; they are practicing adoration, not solving equations or selling soap. When we enter into courtship and marriage we use this language yet again, finding that it is the only language adequate to the reality of our passions and commitments. Romantic love extends and deepens it for as long as we have the will to pursue it. But our will commonly falters, and in the traffic of the everyday and press of making a living, we content ourselves with the required and easier languages of information and motivation. In the early months of parenting, the basic language is relearned and used for awhile. At death, if we know we are dying, we will use nothing else. A few people never quit using it—a few lovers, some poets, the saints—but most let it drift into disuse; Walter Wangerin, Jr. calls this a "vast massacre of neglect."[4]

First Language

Language I is the language of the Psalms and the language of prayer. Not exclusively, of course, for all the languages blend together in actual use, but mostly. It is the language we use naturally at and around the great nodal points of human life when our being is emergent or centered or questioned or endangered. But because it is the language that requires the most of us and hardly anyone (often no one) requires it of us, it is the language in which we are least proficient. It is necessary to acquire Language II if we are to pass from one school grade to the next, and it is gratifying to use Language III to get our own way, but, except for our children, our parents, our lovers, and our God (and altogether they do not add up to very many, and we can easily avoid them if we wish), no one cares overmuch whether we use Language I. And yet this is the language most necessary to our humanity, to finding out who we are and who we are with, for love and for care. And for God.

Languages II and III are no less important in the life of faith but if they are not embedded in Language I they become thin and gaunt—Language II reduced to list making instead of, like Adam, heuristically naming the creatures in the Garden; Language III reduced to crass manipulations instead of, like God in Genesis and Jesus in the Gospels (and all true poets since), creating what is recognized as good.

Because we are more at home in the languages that describe

where we are and get us what we want, and because these languages are more honored in our culture, our habit is to pray in these more easily handled languages. This is fatal to prayer. Informational language is not prayer language. Motivational language is not prayer language. To pray in these languages is, in effect, not to pray. We must let the Psalms train us in prayer language—the language of intimacy, of relationship, of "I and Thou," of personal love.[5]

While it is difficult to acquire proficiency in this language because the time in which we live gives us so little occasion to practice it (like trying to learn French while living in Japan), it is possible for anyone, for it is the first language we all learned. Learning to pray is not learning anything new; it recovers our first language. Developing skill in Language I is a matter of returning to what is basic in us. Prayer is not a second language; it is the language at the core of what we already are and are becoming.

Accurate Prayer

Psalm 3, the first actual prayer in the Psalms, immerses us in Language I. The opening cry, "O Lord, how many are my foes!" swiftly modulates into a lyric of trust, "But thou, O Lord, art a shield about me, my glory, and the lifter of my head." The trouble that provokes the prayer is personal: enemies threaten my life. I experience the enmity in three dimensions: enemies are numerous, overwhelming me with their size ("how many are my foes"); enemies are aggressive, making my situation urgent ("many are rising against me"); and enemies are mocking, debunking my faith and demoralizing my spirit ("saying of me, There is no help for him in God"). The three dimensions of the trouble are matched by a salvation experienced in the same three dimensions: God covers my raw vulnerability as a shield; the contemptuous scorn of enemy taunts is countered by the experience of God as "my glory"; the rise of enmity (this is no passive background hostility but a towering oppression under which my head sinks in discouragement) is reversed by the experience of God raising my head in hope. The cry for help is answered in actions.

At the center of the prayer (vv. 5–6) is an anecdote: a person lies down, falls asleep, and rises again, unafraid even though surrounded by ten thousand enemies. The language is artless, a cameo center. Three verbs describe what everyone does each evening, night, and morning—lie down, go to sleep, get up. These actions are prayer.

Then: "Rise, Lord, save me, O God" (v. 7). Two imperatives seek to change the course of events. The imperative is the verb in its purest form: a call for the action that will change the world, or at least that part of the world that I care about. It is also a confession of inadequacy. Imperatives call to another to do for me what I cannot do for myself. (Imperatives can also be used manipulatively, commanding another to do what I am too lazy to do for myself, but that is a perversion of the form). The entire theology of prayer, that the world and I can be changed and that God is the one to do it, is carried grammatically in the imperative. The verbal mood of prayer runs heavily to imperatives.

A pair of indicatives follow the two imperatives: "thou dost smite all my enemies on the cheek, thou dost break the teeth of the wicked." The intense feeling in these words is exceeded only by their brutality. The violent language of the Psalms has a New Testament equivalent in the Revelation of St. John. This is disturbing. But the first requirement of the language is not to make us nice but accurate. Prayer is not particularly "nice." There is a recognition in prayer of the fiercer aspects of God. Is there anger to be expressed? Are there judgments to be reckoned with? What words are available to say them? That God slaps cheeks and breaks teeth is not theological dogma but prayed metaphor, images that connect experience with eschatology (the God-pull into God's future). Psalm language is not careful about offending our sensibilities; its genius is its complete disclosure of the human spirit as it makes response to the revealing God. Given the mess that things are in, it will not be surprising that some unpleasant matters have to be spoken, and spoken in the language of our sin-conditioned humanity, for the language of prayer is, most emphatically, human language. It is not angel talk.

In the practice of prayer, cries for help get arranged in polarity to a choir of thanks. The last sentence in this prayer is a double exclamation, "Deliverance belongs to the Lord; thy blessing be upon thy people!" (v. 8). In trouble we pray; in the course of the praying our experience of wrong becomes an experience of right, which is even more elemental than wrong, but to which our unprayed experience does not give us as immediate access. Gratitude and well-being get expressed with the same spontaneous accuracy in which we cry out pain, anger, guilt, and terror.

There is not an abstract word in this prayer. The nouns are specific; the verbs are direct. Everything is personal: God is personal, the pray-er is personal, experience is immediate, relationship is central, the emotions of terror and trust are expressed with force. Language I. This is the elemental language we always use when our life, our well-being, and deepest interests— identity, health, love, guilt, trust—are at stake. There is no mere information about God here. There is no program implemented for God here. This is a cry for survival that develops into the shout of the saved.

Elemental is not elementary. The elemental develops in other Psalms into polished liturgies of lament and hymns of praise, lyric songs and honed wisdom. But it all gets its start in the time of trouble, pain in body or soul that finds a way to give thanks. The germ is always in the elemental monosyllables of "Help!" and "thanks!"

Conversion of Language

The Psalms train us in a conversion of language, from talking *about* God to talking *to* God. St. Anselm's critical rewriting of his theology is a landmark instance of the conversion of language for which the Psalms provide the means. He had written his

Monologion, setting forth the proofs of God's existence with great brilliance and power. It is one of the stellar theological achievements in the West. Then he realized that however many right things he had said about God, he had said them all in the wrong language. He rewrote it all in his *Proslogion,* converting his Language II into Language I: first person address, an answer to God, a personal conversation with a personal God. The *Proslogion* is theology as prayer.[6]

We don't quit using the languages of information and motivation when we pray. Competency in all languages is necessary in this life of faith that draws all levels of existence into the service and glory of God. But at or near the center of our lives, where God and the human, faith and the absurd, love and indifference are tangled in daily traffic jams, the language in which we must become proficient is the language of personal relationship, getting as much of our language as possible into the speech of love and response and intimacy: "Abba! Father!"

I have passed out of mind like one who is dead;
   I have become like a broken vessel.
Yea, I hear the whispering of many—
   terror on every side!—
as they scheme together against me,
   as they plot to take my life.
But I trust in thee, O Lord,
   I say, "Thou art my God."
My times are in thy hand.

PSALM 31:12-15

Behold, we are going up to Jerusalem; and the Son of man will be delivered to the chief priests and scribes, and they will condemn him to death, and deliver him to the Gentiles to be mocked and scourged and crucified, and he will be raised on the third day.

JESUS (MATTHEW 20:18-19)

The need is . . . For credible news that our lives proceed in order toward a pattern which, if tragic here and now, is ultimately pleasing in the mind of a god who sees a totality and *at last* enacts His will. We crave nothing less than perfect story; and while we chatter or listen all our lives in a din of craving—jokes, anecdotes, novels, dreams, films, plays, songs, half the words of our days—we are satisfied only by the one short tale we feel to be true.

REYNOLDS PRICE

4. Story

The first actual prayer in the Psalms, Psalm 3, is introduced by a phrase that splices it into a piece of history: "A Psalm of David, when he fled from Absalom his son." All who read scripture know this story well, and the single, unadorned sentence triggers its recall. Absalom instigated a palace coup and David fled for his life to the wilderness. Civil war followed, father fighting son, son fighting father. David won back his throne at a terrible cost, the death of his son, over which he mourned magnificently.

The life of David is full of incidents like this. Everyone's life is. Not a palace coup for most of us and, hopefully, not the treachery of a son, but conflict and failure and fear, love and betrayal, loss and salvation. Every day is a story, a morning beginning and evening ending that are boundaries for people who go about their tasks with more or less purpose, go to war, make love, earn a living, scheme and sin and believe. Everything is connected. Meaning is everywhere. The days add up to a life that is a story.

Psalm 3, its title tells us, is prayed in the middle of a story. All prayer is prayed in a story, by someone who is in the story. There are no storyless prayers. Story is to prayer what the body is to the soul, the circumstances in which it takes place. And prayer is to story what the soul is to the body, the life without which it would be a corpse. Prayers are prayed by people who live stories. Every life is a story. We are not always aware that we are living a story; often it seems more like a laundry list. But story it is.

The Editorial Connection

Most of the Psalms have an introductory sentence that inserts them into a story. Only thirty-four do not. Sometimes the reference makes a clear connection with a familiar biblical narrative. Sometimes it is obscure, giving instructions, no longer clear to us, on how it is to be used or sung in worship, the most important activity in Israel's story. But either way, as a link to someone's life (usually David's) or as instruction for Israel's temple worship, the sentence ties the prayer to the historical: place, time, people. Prayer is connected by these titles to a world of friends and enemies, sickness and health, song and celebration.

Interestingly, none of these psalm titles tells us anything about the origin of the psalm. They were all affixed at some later date by editors, whose names we do not know. For a hundred years now, the scholars who have given devout attention to the Psalms have agreed on this—an impressive consensus. David certainly wrote some of them, but we don't know for sure which ones. It is a disappointment to learn that we don't know who wrote the Psalms, or the circumstances of those who wrote them. But the disappointment has a compensation: we know more than ever how they were used. The Psalms show Israel, our ancestral people of God, at worship. They show the shape of this worshiping community in all its astonishing vitality and variety. If we know less than we once thought we did about who wrote them and why they were written, we know more about the way and circumstances in which they were prayed, and praying them, not investigating them, is the Christian's main business.

But why, then, the titles? What use do they serve? If they are the work of the psalm editors and not the psalm writers, shouldn't we ignore them and get on with what we know is authentic, the psalms themselves? But editorial work in the Psalms, while subsequent to composition, is never secondary; it is integral to the formation of our primary text for prayer. What the psalm editors did is as significant for the life of prayer as what the psalm writers did. We have seen the importance of the editorially placed Psalms 1 and 2 in preparing us for prayer. This second editorial activity, placing titles on 116 of the psalms, is of comparable importance, protecting us from the common and fatal error of spiritualized prayer.

The David Story

Spiritualized prayer is denatured prayer, prayer in which all the dirt and noise of ordinary life is boiled out. It is a prayer that cultivates exalted feelings and sublime thoughts. It is prayer that is embarrassed by the coarse subject matter that intrudes itself into most twenty-four hour periods, but takes great pleasure in grand aphorisms. It is escapist prayer, with scheduled flights to the empyrean.

The psalms editors, knowing our weakness for these fantasies, use titles to tie the balloon of prayer to people in a story: for life is always and necessarily lived in detail, and the details are often inconvenient and irregular. The most common tie is simply "of David." Seventy-three psalms are so identified: "A Psalm of David," or "A Psalm for David," or "A Psalm in the tradition of David." The Hebrew, *l'dawid*, is not precise. Some were written by him, others written in honor of him, most written in awareness of him. He was the most prominent of all who wrote prayers in Israel. He was remembered by all as the "sweet psalmist of Israel."

It is a particularly happy identification, for David's life is the most exuberant life story in all the scriptures, maybe the most exuberant in all world history. It is also the most extensively narrated story in our Bible. We know more about David than any other person in the biblical communities of faith. We are given David in his youth, his adulthood, and his old age. We are given stories of his life in singleness and marriage, his conduct in war and peace, his splendid holiness and sordid sin, his friendships and betrayals, his terrific triumphs and heartbreaking tragedies. The entire breathtaking sweep of the human condition stretches its horizons in this David. There is no part of our lives that does not find some point of illumination or encouragement or rebuke in this life story.

The person in scripture who has the most extensively told story is the same person who is shown to be most at prayer. The outside of his life is told in story, the inside is told in prayer. The books of Samuel and Chronicles give the plot to David's story, the Psalms show the passion. There is a sense in which we can be spectators to the narratives of our own lives, detached and gossipy. Prayer is a way in, the way to receive and deepen the meaning of the narrative. Faith is the most interior of human acts. Prayer is the means by which holiness/health is grafted into the unfaithful parts, inserted into the empty parts.

Also, and this is important for people who pray, David was a lay person. He was neither prophet, priest, or wise man (the three religious vocations of his time). He was a shepherd, guerrilla fighter, court musician, and politician. His entire life was lived in the sacred ordinary that we are apt, mistakenly, to call the secular. The regular place of prayer is the ordinary life.

Of the seventy-three psalms that are linked to David's story, thirteen refer to specific incidents in his life. These references pull into focused clarity various parts of the story of this person who has a "heart after God," which is what people at prayer are trying to nurture.

Psalm 3: When he fled from Absalom his son.
Psalm 7: Which he sang to the Lord concerning Cush, a Benjaminite.
Psalm 18: When the Lord delivered him from the hand of all his enemies, and from the hand of Saul.
Psalm 34: When he feigned madness before Abimelech, so that he drove him out, and he went away.
Psalm 51: When Nathan the prophet came to him, after he had gone in to Bathsheba.
Psalm 52: When Doeg, the Edomite, came and told Saul, "David has come to the house of Ahimelech."
Psalm 54: When the Ziphites went and told Saul, "David is in hiding among us."
Psalm 56: When the Philistines seized him in Gath.
Psalm 57: When he fled from Saul, in the cave.

Psalm 59: When Saul sent men to watch his house in order to kill him.

Psalm 60: When he strove with Aram-naharaim and with Aram-zobah, and when Joab on his return killed twelve thousand of Edom in the Valley of Salt.

Psalm 63: When he was in the Wilderness of Judah.

Psalm 142: When he was in the cave.

Two things stand out in this list. First, each incident is a time of trouble. There is not a single royal psalm representing the kingly office. (Psalm 18 is only a partial exception). The parts of David's life that are recalled are those in which he is struggling through the dark passages of all human beings. This confirms our earlier conviction that prayer begins in trouble. We pray out of need. There is plenty of praise in these prayers, but it is trouble that gets the prayer started. The editorial instinct of our prayer masters was to tie prayer to the place of trouble. We are now over one hurdle: if we ever thought that escape from the troublesome was the route to prayer, these titles have cured us.

Second: the list is random. There is no attempt to connect every psalm with an incident in David's life, either to prove to the last detail that David prayed in each incident, or to demonstrate that prayer is appropriate in all circumstances. The seventeen psalm titles are pump priming. They get us started. They show what is possible. They do not do all our work for us. Now, it is up to us to insert them in our stories.

The psalm titles tug at our attention, saying, "Remember, this is a *story* you are in. By praying you do not get out of the difficult work of sin and enemy and family, you get further into it. Instead of finding it easier, you will find it more demanding. You will not become spiritualized and above it all. You are no longer exterior; you are an insider to yourself, to others, and to God."

The people who studied and prayed the Psalms continued this "storying." Eventually every psalm was provided with a historical setting in someone's life (but most commonly David's) by Jewish and Christian commentators. The impulse to insert prayer into story was strong, and at the end, all the prayers were gathered under David's aegis, including the psalms attributed to Moses, Solomon, and a few others. "David came to be regarded as the source of Israel's psalms as Moses was for the law, and Solomon was for wisdom."[1] In ancient Hebrew manuscripts of the books of Samuel, spaces were left where readers could consider a psalm that was relevant to that aspect of the life of David.[2] By means of this insistent, thoroughgoing connection with David's story, the Psalms have become immediately accessible to all stories. We are given a feel for the "fringes and hollows of life in which life is lived,"[3]—where prayer, by embracing each odd and local particularity, matures. Through the human mouth of David, they become a personal word provided by God for each human situation. Conceivably, the titles could have tied the psalms to the ancient past in such a way as to separate them from us. The opposite happened. Prayer was humanized and historized for every individual.

The Big Story

We read on in the Psalms. It is not long before we arrive at a third sign of editorial work. At the end of Psalm 41 we read: "Blessed be the Lord, the God of Israel, from everlasting to everlasting! Amen and Amen." It reads like a conclusion, but it is not because other psalms follow. We keep reading and find, at the end of Psalm 72, "The prayers of David are ended." That also sounds like a conclusion, but psalms continue. We come across two more conclusions (89:52 and 106:48) before Psalm 150 definitively closes the collection. We count up the conclusions. There are five. The 150 psalms are arranged into five "books." What are the editors doing? The term "editors" is misleading. "Spiritual masters" is more like it. They wisely shaped the text of prayer so that it would form healthy lives of prayer. We discern devout intelligences at work protecting us against another common error, presumptuous prayer.

Presumptuous prayer speaks to God without first listening to him. It obsessively, anxiously, or pretentiously multiplies human words to God, but with, at best, a distracted, indifferent, or fitful interest in God's words to us. But God speaks to us before we speak to him. If we pray without listening, we pray out of context.

Protection against presumption comes in the editorial arrangement of the psalms into five books, showing that prayer is a response to the Torah's five books. The narrative of our lives received its classic form in the five books of Torah: Genesis, Exodus, Leviticus, Numbers, and Deuteronomy. Life from its inception (Genesis) to its fulfillment (Deuteronomy) is the result of God's making, redeeming, providing, and blessing word. God's word is authorizing—an author at work: the world and our lives are given narrative shape; story is brought into existence with salvation as its plot. So we need to pray not only out of an awareness of our personal stories (that David's life gives us), but in the context of the "old, old story," the salvation story. Our daily lives have narrative shape, but the Bible as a whole (the large context in which we live) is also cast in the form of narrative.

Language, by its very nature, is not monologue but dialogue. God does not impose his plot of salvation on the people in his story. He speaks in order to be answered. The character of each person in the story (and we are all in it) is allowed to form from the inside, in the give and take of dialogue, each with its own rhythms, at its own pace. We are in a world of salvation in which God is speaking to us. How do we answer? We are not good at this language. The Psalms instruct, train, immerse us in the answering speech which is our part in the exchange of words by which our being in the image of God and redemption by the blood of Christ is formed internally into maturity.

"Moses" sets out the word of God that calls us: calls us into being, to judgment, into salvation. "David" gives us our answering call: calling to God in trust, protest, lament, praise. The Psalms in five books are antiphonal to the Torah in five books. Five is matched by five, like the fingers of clasped and praying hands.

Prayer is everywhere and always answering speech. It is never initiating speech, and to suppose that it is presumptuous. *Miqra,* the Hebrew word for Bible, properly means "calling out "—the calling out of God to us. "God must become a person," but in order for us to speak in answer to him he must make us into persons. We become ourselves as we answer, sometimes angrily disputing with him about how he rules the world, sometimes humbling ourselves before him in grateful trust. Prayer is language used to respond to the most that has been said to us, with the potential for saying all that is in us. Prayer is the development of speech into maturity, the language that is adequate to answering the one who has spoken comprehensively to us. Prayer is not a narrow use of language for speciality occasions, but language catholic, embracing the totality of everything and everyone everywhere. This conversation is both bold and devout—the utterly inferior responding to the utterly superior. In this exchange we become persons. The entire life of faith is dialogue. By means of the Psalms we find our voice in the dialogue. In prayer we do not merely speak our feelings, we speak our answers. We can answer, we are permitted to answer. If we truly answer God there is nothing that we may not say to him.[4]

But note well: stock answers are not prescribed. There is no verse by verse correspondence between the first book of Torah and the first book of Psalms. The editorial arrangement does not give us a phrase book of rote answers of Psalm 19, say, to answer Genesis 19. What we have, rather, is a listening and answering context with an immersion in language adequate to the dialogue. Catechism answers will not serve, for that is not the way conversation takes place between living persons. We acquire facility in personal language that is accurately responsive out of our changing lives and growing levels of faith to what God speaks to us in scripture and in Christ. We need a vocabulary and syntax sufficiently personal and adequately wide-ranging to answer everything that God says.

This unobtrusive, five-book arrangement is quietly but insistently provided to protect us against a presumption, whether inadvertent or willful, to pray in any other way than by listening and answering to God's word.

The Unique Story

There is a kind of storytelling that relies exclusively on the manipulation of plot to get its effects. In such stories there is no development of character and no cultivation of atmosphere. Everything is exterior: form, incident, action. A clever writer can write the same book over and over again, with slight plot alterations, and please millions of lazy people with stories of spies, lovers, detectives, and space travelers. Real writers don't do this. They work from the inside, discovering the way the world is, patiently uncovering the slow growth of personality, the long and subtle changes that sin works in the mind, the secret movements of grace. These writers don't impose themselves on their material, or take shortcuts for cheap effects.

There is also a kind of religious exhortation that tells the gospel story in stereotypes—a kind of salvation according to James Bond. Gaudy combinations of slogan and suggestion that promise diversion from boredom and omit mention of the demanding interiorizing of faith. They appeal to the adolescent in us without involving us in the pain growing up. In adolescence the form of adulthood is reached several years ahead of the substance. For a few years, all adolescents look and act and talk more or less alike. They have not had time to develop their insides. That takes years and years. Many never to it. There is nothing wrong with being an adolescent. There are moments when it is almost wonderful, but it is grotesque to remain one. Form is essential, but if it is not filled with content, it is finally false. But the filling takes time. These people profess the story form of salvation, but fail to fill it, or let it be filled with prayer. They end up all plot and no character.

Our interiors must develop along with our exteriors. The story of salvation has predictable outlines, but the individual character of the saved person is never predictable. That is always unique. The uniqueness is carved by prayer. We would like, if the Spirit would allow it, to interiorize only random bits and pieces of our lives on the occasions when we felt like it. The Psalms do not permit that—they are a rigorous interiorization of everything, the gamut of the human condition, in the story of salvation.

Story making is creative work—demanding intense and personal involvement. The most common alternative to story in our culture is the journalistic report, which coolly stands apart from the personal and delivers information to us so that we can read it in a safe place. Another common alternative is the work agenda and its sequel, the work report, which list the activities of our day with no connection with who we are. A robot, if sophisticated enough, could stand in for us. The journalist uses words that require the use of our minds; the job foreman uses words that require the use of our bodies; the story maker enlists our imagination, the interiorization and integration of body and mind, which puts us on the threshold of prayer.

God works with words. He uses them to make a story of salvation. He pulls us into the story. When we believe, we become willing participants in the plot. We can do this reluctantly and minimally, going through the motions; or we can do it recklessly and robustly, throwing ourselves into the relationships and actions. When we do this, we pray. We practice the words and phrases that make us fluent in the conversation that is at the center of the story. We develop the free responses that answer to the creating word of God in and around us that is making a salvation story.

Thou hast made the moon to mark the seasons;
    the sun knows its time for setting.
Thou makest darkness, and it is night,
    when all the beasts of the forest creep forth.
The young lions roar for their prey,
    seeking their food from God.
When the sun rises, they get them away
    and lie down in their dens.
Man goes forth to his work
    and to his labor until the evening.

PSALM 104:19–23

Come to me, all who labor and are heavy laden, and I will give you rest. Take my yoke upon you, and learn from me; for I am gentle and lowly in heart, and you will find rest for your souls. For my yoke is easy, and my burden is light.

JESUS (MATTHEW 11:28–30)

"The lack of synchronicity between nature and man caused the lack of synchronicity between body and soul. When the nightingale isn't heard, the Molotov cocktail is."

ODYSSEAS ELYTIS

5. Rhythm

The pre-Genesis condition of the cosmos is our own inner life: *tohu* and *bohu*, without form and void. Things are not right; *we* are not right. Our emotions bolt and stampede. Our thoughts run riot. Our bodies hurt. Our appetites play havoc with our virtue. We can't, it seems, direct our own destiny with dignity or wisdom for ten consecutive minutes.

And so we pray. Directed by the Psalms, we begin our praying by listening. What do we hear?

> And God said, Let there be light. . . .
> And there was evening and there was morning, one day.
> And God said, Let there be a firmament. . . .
> And there was evening and there was morning, a second day.
> And God said, Let the waters . . . be gathered together. . . .
> And there was evening and there was morning, a third day.
> And God said, Let there be lights in the firmament. . . .
> And there was evening and there was morning, a fourth day.
> And God said, Let the waters bring forth swarms of living
> creatures. . . .
> And there was evening and there was morning, a fifth day.
> And God said, let the earth bring forth living creatures. . . .
> And there was evening and there was morning, a sixth day.

Disorder gives way, piecemeal, to order. Chaos becomes cosmos. The language is rhythmic—cadence and repetition and rhyme. God speaks creation into existence: "He spoke and it came to be; he commanded and it stood forth" (Ps. 33:9). The rhythmic language makes a rhythmic creation.

We both live and speak rhythmically. Rhythm is embedded in our bodies and in our world. The rhythms are contrapuntal, pulse counterpointed to seasons, breathing to moon phases. We live and speak in a fugue.

Poetry takes the natural rhythms of language and deepens them, fitting sounds and meanings into the interior rhythms of our breathing and pulse, and then extends them to the environmental rhythms of days, months, and years. "Rhythm," John Ciardi once said, "shakes language down into the nervous system."[1]

All the psalms are given to us in the form of poetry. Prayer is rhythmic, using language to integrate our blessings to our breathing, adjusting the internal rhythms of our lives to the external rhythms of creation and covenant. Our core being is expressed in language that follows the rhythms of our life, inhalation and exhalation. We cannot breathe out what we have not first breathed in. The breath that God breathes into us in daily pentecosts, is breathed out in our prayers, "telling in our own tongues the mighty works of God" (Acts 2:11). We can, of course, pray in a frenzy, thrashing about. Much prayer necessarily begins that way, but we pray better, and best, when we let the rhythms of the creating word of God work themselves into the rhythms of our living, and then find expression in the psalmic rhythms of prayer.

Evening and Morning

The most conspicuous immediate effect of this is to slow down our prayers: we cannot speed-read a poem. Poetry cannot be hurried. We must slow our minds (and in prayer, our lives) to the pace of the poet's breathing, phrases separated by pauses. Hermann Gunkel, the pioneer Psalms scholar, "always insisted that the text be read aloud in order that the reader might better discern its movement and direction, its rhythms and assonance, its key words and accents. He knew how to *listen* to a text."[2]

Poetry requires equal time be given to sounds and silences. In all language silence is as important as sound. But more often than not we are merely impatient with the silence. Mobs of words run out of our mouths, nonstop, trampling the grassy and sacred silence. We stop only when breathless. Why do we talk so much? Why do we talk so fast? Hurry is a form of violence practiced on time. But time is sacred. The purpose of language is not to murder the silence but to enter it, cautiously and reverently. The poet carefully arranges words in settings of silence, letting the sounds resonate, the meanings vibrate. Silence is not what is left over when there is nothing more to say but the aspect of time that gives meaning to sound. The poem restores silence to language so that words, organic and living, once again are given time to pulse and breathe.

Before we open our mouths in prayer, our open ears take in words that form light and coherence within us, goodness and blessing, and best of all, the image of God. Our jerky rebellion and spastic ignorance is absorbed into the rhythms of "And God said. . . . And it was so," and into the resultant rhythms of creation, "evening and morning . . . evening and morning . . . evening and morning. . .," sleeping and waking.

These rhythms train us in prayers that are tidal—oceanic prayers gathering much more beneath and beyond them than anything we are aware of from our place on the beach.

Evening Prayer

Psalm 4, an evening prayer, and Psalm 5, a morning prayer, are strategically placed by our prayer masters early in our text to establish these fundamental rhythms in our lives and get us praying in the cadence of God's word. The rhythm of breathing in and breathing out is now integrated into the rhythm of going to sleep and waking up, and prayers formed on these rhythms coordinate the deeply personal with the deep purposes of God as he speaks his love into being in us, "The love that moves the sun and the other stars,"[3] and "Deep calls to deep" (Ps. 42:7).

It is first evening prayer, then morning prayer. The order is not reversible. Evening prayer is succeeded, after several hours of unconsciousness, by morning prayer. The sequence is not Hebrew perversity but grace embedded in the earth's rotation.

We assimilate the Genesis rhythms, language in which God

brings his will into being in rock, protoplasm, sun, and sea, believing that an identical language brings his will into being in bodies and souls, in sin and out of evil. Prayer is not a frill; it articulates the primordial in us. It submits to the "darkness on the face of the deep" and wakes us to Lord's Day light. Everyone sleeps. Everyone wakes. Out of these aboriginal states, we realize the will of our Creator and Redeemer worked in us. Sleeping and waking are theological as well as biological. The bodily conditions are also spiritual modes.

Psalm 4 marks the transition from the daylight world, in which it is easy to suppose that we are in control, to the night world in which we relinquish our grip on jobs, people, even thoughts, and experience the will that is greater than ours, the God who answers previous to our asking, who acts previous to our prompting.

We begin our lives asleep in the womb, formed by another. Passive in the darkness, we are made. When we finally venture into daylight action, we are not done with the passivities of sleep, but return to them at once. In our early days we are more asleep than awake, as another, and others nourish us into the wholeness that we have neither the wisdom nor the strength to fashion for ourselves. Gradually, our waking hours lengthen and we take up for ourselves tasks others did for us, entering into the work of the world—loving, helping, feeding, healing, building, teaching, making. But we never arrive at a condition where we are beyond sleep, self-sufficient in twenty-four-hour control. Daily we give up consciousness, submitting ourselves to that which is deeper than consciousness in order to grow and be healed, be created and saved. Going to sleep is biological necessity; it can also be an act of faith. People who live by faith have always welcomed the evening hour for prayer, disengaging themselves from the discordant, arhythmic confusion of tongues, and sinking into the quiet rhythms of God's creating and covenanting words.

Even though it is decreed in our bodies that we return to this sleep, it is not easy. We want to stay in control. We want to over-see the operation. Evening prayer is a deliberate act of spirit that cultivates willingly what our bodies force on us finally.[4]

From the clamorous beginning, "Answer me when I call, O God of my right! (v. 1) to the quiet conclusion, "In peace I will both lie down and sleep; for thou alone, O Lord, makest me dwell in safety," (v. 8) this evening prayer is a symmetrical beau-ty, arranging two sets of contrasts on either side of a center that uses six verbs to restore the rhythms of grace in us.

The first contrast is between those who pursue futility (v. 2) and those who realize providence (v. 3). Some people, deceived by their own hearts and the devil's illusions, fill the day with a desperate and anxious grasp for that which is not. Others dis-cover God's providential motions in themselves and others. Ob-serving and reflecting on this contrast releases us from futility and relaxes us into grace.

The second contrast is between those who are perpetually ask-ing God for what they do not have (v. 6) and those who are over-whelmed before God with what he has already given (v. 7). St. Francis de Sales divided the population similarly: the immature who are unhappy over what they don't have, and the mature who are happy with what they do have.[5]

But the center of the prayer is definitive: six paired verbs move us from self-assertion in which we push our vain wills on the people and circumstances around us—acting as if we are in charge of the universe—to a believing obedience that acts as if God is in charge and that submits to becoming the kind of per-son that God is in charge of.

"Be angry." No day is perfect. Things go wrong. Some things always go wrong, many of them out of spite, malice, and blas-phemy. Face squarely the worst of the day, and be angry. Don't make excuses for yourself or others. Don't paper over any flaws. You do well to be angry. "But sin not." Your anger is not a work agenda for you to plan a vengeance that will fix the wrong. What is wrong with the world is God's business. It is a business in which you will have a part, come morning when you get your assignment. Meanwhile God is giving help at a far deeper level than any of your meddling will ever reach.

"Commune with your own hearts on your beds." Speak to yourself. Listen to yourself. In the crossfire of daytime voices, we become strangers to ourselves. Get acquainted again with the being that God created, not just the passport version that you have used to get more or less successfully through the day. *"And be silent."* Nothing more need be said. No explanations, no boasts, no apologies. This is who you are. There is something more important than liking or not liking yourself, more significant than the day's accomplishments and failures; there is *you*. In the silence, simply be the person that God is gathering into salvation.

"Offer right sacrifices." A sacrifice is an offering placed before the Lord so that he can make something of it. Once offered it is in God's hand to do with what he will. It is no longer in your hands to improve a little more. You have had all day, now let God have all night. His will is to work with your offerings, not your perfections or your press clippings. Just leave it. You have lived your day; now leave it on the altar, an offering. *"And put your trust in the Lord."* We have considerable evidence of what God does with our offerings—he transforms them. On Hebrew altars the change was visible in the purificatory burning, a fragrant and smoky ascent into heaven. In the Christian eucharist the bread and wine offered are received back as the flesh and blood of Christ. The change involves forgiveness and sanctification: a sinful life is offered up, a holy life is received back.

Low tide. We sleep.

Morning Prayer

Psalm 5 prays our reentry into the waking world's daylight. Every morning is a wonder: "What has really happened during the last seven days and nights? Seven times we have been dissolved into darkness as we shall be dissolved into dust; our very selves, so far as we know, have been wiped out of the world of living things; and seven times we have been raised alive like Lazarus, and found all our limbs and senses unaltered, with the coming of the day."[6]

When we open our eyes, the day is half-over. While we have been sleeping, God has been working. We wake into a world in which God's word has been making aspens and salamanders and puppies. We open our eyes and see what he has brought out of darkness: light. And life.

Everyone, of course, wakes. We open our eyes. We stretch our limbs. And then what? If we are to sustain the rhythms established in our sleeping, we answer the word of God that has brought us into being and into the light, and pray God to listen to our answer: "Give ear. . . . give heed. . . . Hearken. . . . for to thee do I pray." The quartet of verbs in the opening lines of Psalm 5 harmonize an expectation that God will listen. "True prayer is sure of a hearing. . . . We can doubt the value, power and sincerity of our own asking, but not God's hearing. . . . It is because it is heard that we pray, and not because we are so skilled in asking."[7]

Morning prayer prepares for action. Passivity, in which we let God work his will in us, is primary, but activity, in which we obey the will worked in us in the world, is also essential. But our activities must be continuous with our passivities. We must not foolishly abandon what we experience in sleep when we awake into action. Psalm 5 bridges the passivities of grace into the activities of obedience. It is a narrow bridge easily missed, even more easily fallen off.

The daylight world of action is perilous. Psalm 5 trains us to discern and discriminate. It does this by contrasting the possibilities for evil action (vv. 4–6) and obedient action (vv. 7–8), and then repeats the contrast: liars and flatters (vv. 9–10) contrasted with singers and lovers (vv. 11–12). Seven of the attributions of evil activity refer to its verbal aspects ("the boastful," "those who speak lies," "deceitful men," "no truth in their mouth," "throat is an open sepulcher," "flatter with their tongue," "our counsels"). We live by words: by words God speaks to us, by words we pray to him. Words are at the center of the human condition. All the time that God is speaking and we are praying, seductive, flattering, and lying words that incite unbelieving actions infiltrate the language. We had better be alert and not believe everything we hear.

And so we enter the day having conducted a reconnaissance of evil and examined our own hearts for illusions of innocence. Parallel to the reconnaissance is the orientation to sacred time and space and holy good pleasure. We also know something of holiness.

The controlling center of this morning prayer is v. 3: "O Lord, in the morning, thou dost hear my voice: in the morning, I prepare a sacrifice for thee, and watch." The image of bringing a sacrifice is a rhythmic repetition from the evening prayer (4:5).

The work of God begins while we are asleep and without our help. He continues to work through the day in our worship and obedience. A sacrifice is the material means of assembling a life before God in order to let God work with it. Sacrifice isn't something we do for God, but simply setting out the stuff of life for him to do something with. On the altar the sacrificial offering is changed into what is pleasing and acceptable to God. In the act of offering we give up ownership and control, and watch to see what God will do with it. With a deep awareness that the God who speaks life into us also listens when we speak, we put into words the difficulties and delights that we foresee in the hours ahead. We assemble fears and hopes, apprehensions and anticipations, and place them on the altar as an offering: "I prepare a sacrifice, and watch."

Watch is the pivotal word in morning prayer. A biblically trained ear hears a story in the word. Jacob, fleeing from his father-in-law Laban, was caught in Gilead. Laban thought he had been defrauded by Jacob; Jacob was sure he had been gypped by Laban. In Gilead, through argument and prayer, they came to an agreement. They set up an altar pillar and ate a covenantal meal before it. They named the pillar, "Watching Place" *(Mizpah)*. They had spent twenty years watching each other suspiciously, watching for opportunities to take advantage of each other. Here they agreed to quit watching each other and let God watch them. Early in the morning the two old antagonists parted—Laban returning to Haran and Jacob entering Canaan where he still had to face the enmity of his brother Esau—with their morning prayer echoing across the Gilead hills: "The Lord watch between you and me, while we are absent one from the other." Leaving the place of morning prayer and watching, the first things Jacob saw were the angels of God. He exclaimed: "This is God's army!" (Genesis 31).

Mizpah is a borderline experience repeated as often as every morning. We watch to see what God will do with the assemblage of hopes and fears we set before him. Morning prayer places us before the watchful God and readies us to enter the day watchful, watching our dangerous past recede, watching the dangerous day fill with God's angels. High tide.

The Lord is my rock, and my fortress, and my deliverer,
　　my God, my rock, in whom I take refuge,
my shield, and the horn of my salvation, my stronghold.

PSALM 18:2

I am the bread of life; he who comes to me shall not hunger,
and he who believes in me shall never thirst.

JESUS (JOHN 6:35)

Metaphors are very strange because when you put two things
together it's a way of discovering meanings which haven't
been discovered before.

WALKER PERCY

6. Metaphor

John Calvin frequently referred to the world around us as a "theater of God's glory."[1] We write of the Creator's dazzling performance in putting together the elements of matter and arranging the components of the cosmos. Everything is created. Everything carries within its form and texture the signature of its Creator. No part of this material world is unconnected with God; every cell is in the organism of salvation. Biblical religion cannot be lived apart from matter—the seen, felt, tasted, smelled, and listened to creation.

It is all, precisely, *creation*. Nothing merely happened along. Chokecherries and tundra and weasels are not random accidents. Since everything is by design, no part of creation can be bypassed if we intend to live in the fullest possible relation to our Creator in his creation. None of it is an inconvenience that we are forced to put up with. Nothing is a stumbling block introduced by the devil to trip the feet of those whose eyes are piously lifted in praise to God. Creation is our place for meeting God and conversing with him. The voice that spoke Behemoth and Leviathan into being is the same voice that says, "Your sins are forgiven you," and invites us to call upon him in the day of trouble. External and internal are the same reality. Heaven and earth are formed by a single will of God.

We take box seats in this creation theater when we pray. We look around. The mountains are huge, heaving their bulk upwards. The creeks spill across the rocks, giving extravagant light shows under the hemlocks. The lakes fill up with sky, on earth as it is in heaven. A lion rips its prey. A sparrow builds its nest. Solomon and the Shulamite embrace. An eagle plummets from a cloud to a meadow and takes a rabbit in its talons; for a few moments the two genesis creatures are in a terrible and tangled harmony. An infant drinks her fill of breakfast from her mother's breast. Matter is real. Flesh is good.

True, there are things wrong in the world, things not easy to understand. It is impossible to account for the presence of the mosquito and leukemia. Parasites make up ten percent of living creatures. Annie Dillard calls them "the devils' tithe."[2] Appalling imbecilities stalk the shadows of the creation theater. Creation is thunderous with its hallelujahs, but we are not around very long before we also hear considerable groaning.

All the same, it is quite definitely a theater in which we behold the glory, not a junk yard of cosmic garbage in which we are bag ladies sorting through the debris, picking out items on which to survive.

The psalmists have season tickets in this theater. All the psalms are prayed in it. They pray breathless in awe, laughing and crying, puzzled and dismayed, complaining and believing. They are not uncritical of what they see and do not scruple to find fault with either author or performance. All is not to their liking, and during some scenes they seem about to walk out. But they do not.

They don't walk out because their business is prayer, and there is no prayer, real prayer, outside the theater. Dissociated from creation, prayer drifts into silly sentimentalism, or snobbish mysticism, or pious elitism. The intent of prayer is not to refine our coarse materiality into pure spirit so that we will not embarrass heaven with the vulgarities of flesh. We are not angels, nor are we to become angels. The Word did not become a good idea, or a numinous feeling, or a moral aspiration: the Word became *flesh* and went on to change water into wine, and then wine into blood. Prayer aids and abets this becoming, taking wispy devotional impulses and making them solid in muscle and bone. Our Lord left us a command to remember and receive him in the act of eating bread and drinking wine. Things matter. The physical is holy. In the opening sentences of the Bible, God spoke a world of energy and matter into being—light, moon, stars, earth, vegetation, fish, birds, man, woman—*not* love and virtue, faith and salvation, hope and judgment, though they will come soon enough. The opening lines of Genesis sound more like minutes copied out in a physics laboratory than in a prayer meeting. But in the Psalms physics and prayer occupy the same space.

The Metaphors of Psalm 18

The dominant diction in this theater is metaphor. Metaphor is the witness of language that spirit and matter are congruent. Metaphor uses the language of sense experience to lead us into the world of the unseen: faith, guilt, mind, God. The visible and invisible, put asunder by sin, are joined by metaphor.

So, when the psalmists pray, they call up lions and snares and dirt to talk about sin, sun and shade and king to address God, tree and mountain and lamb to designate lives blessed by God. There is not a single psalm without its metaphor or metaphors. Metaphor is the characteristic language of prayer. Psalm 18, a bravura cadenza of metaphor, puts the diction on display.

Psalm 18 is a prayer of great vigor, traditionally associated with David as he sums up his life in valedictory praise. At the outset God is addressed as strength, rock, fortress, deliverer, shield, horn, and stronghold. This is followed by a description of extensive personal trouble: cords of death, torrents of perdition, cords of Sheol, snares of death. God responds to the cry for help. His response is fierce: smoke streams from his mouth, he descends from the heavens mantled in darkness under a canopy of rain clouds and mounted on a cherub.. Out of this soaring darkness / brightness, coals-of-fire-hailstones rain destruction, and arrow-lightnings impale evildoers, while an enormous blast of breath from God's nostrils parts the sea and lays bare the world's foundations. And then, abruptly, the metaphors of ferocity give way to one of immense gentleness—God reaches down with his own hand, pulls the one who is praying from the clutch of waters and enemies, and places him on a dry and spacious land, saved.

Later in the prayer, exuberant, the psalmist summarizes his career in the highly improbable but actually experienced country of salvation: "I can," he says "leap over a wall." The metaphor compacts and then explodes energy and grace. And it does not exaggerate.

There is much more in Psalm 18, but that is enough to demonstrate the prominence of metaphor in prayer. In prayer the task is not to rarify language into an abstract spirituality but to thicken it with the metaphors of weather and geography and enmity into a spirituality of honest and actual experience.

What the rhythms of language are to time, the metaphors of language are to place. God speaks to us in time and place. We must, therefore, answer, that is, pray, in time and in place. The rhythms of language are used by the psalmists to develop the cadences of the Genesis day in us; the metaphors of language are used by the psalmists to ground our prayers in the Genesis earth. Without rhythm our prayers have the St. Vitus dance. Without metaphor our prayers are up in the air.

The Gnostic Life

There are always people who talk a good deal about prayer, but don't go near the creation theater. It is not that they don't know about it, or can't afford the price of admission. They stay away on principle. Some of them go so far as to say it is immoral, and urge their young and any others they can influence to stay away also lest they be corrupted by it. A convenient label for these people is *gnostic*. Most gnostics have never heard the word gnostic. Gnostics don't carry membership cards. There have been a few times in history when gnostics formed an identifiable sect and did outright battle with the theater-going church, but for the most part gnosticism is a tilt of soul, a tendency of spirit that doesn't call attention to itself as such. People who pursue excellence with God and decide on a life of prayer are particularly vulnerable to being influenced by it.

The gnostic line is quite convincing when we first come

across it. There is an ascetical earnestness and mystical intensity that catches our attention. Because these people seem to be so deeply concerned about the inner life and to know so much more than anyone else about the graduate levels of spirituality, we are attracted and want to know more. But beware the gnostics: it is difficult to dislike them, harder still to label them, for the forms are protean. A great deal of what they say and do is beautiful. But there are two elements that through their influence insinuate themselves into the prayer of faith. These elements are corrosive and can be fatal: contempt for the material and lust for the secretive. "Gnosticism" says Virginia Stem Owens, "is still the biggest lie of all."[3]

Gnostics despise matter. Most are courteous in their contempt, but their politeness of expression doesn't mitigate their dogma. Matter is, after all, mostly dirty, inconvenient, and an impossible drag on their aspirations to rise into the realm of spirit where they can contemplate pure beauty, truth, and goodness. In the scale of being matter is lower and detracts from what is higher. It is also the evident source of most trouble. If there were no *things*, there would be neither theft nor covetousness. If there were no flesh, there would be neither gluttony nor fornication. The enormous amounts of time that gnostics are required to spend on domestic affairs is wasted on the material—washing dishes, doing laundry, taking out the garbage, mowing the lawn, cleaning out the gutters. It stands to reason (gnostics are big on reason, not quite so ardent in common sense) that the less they are involved in the material the more they can be devoted to the spiritual—appreciating beauty, contemplating truth, cultivating feelings of goodness, and loving the universe. Deep within them they all sense a being that is in exile, a nightingale soul caged in their skeleton of cartilage and bone, and compromised intolerably by the conditions of this passing world.

And gnostics delight in secrecy. They are prototypical insiders. They think that access to the Eternal is by password and that they know the password. They love insider talk and esoteric lore. They elaborate complex myths that account for the descent of our spiritual selves into this messy world of materiality, and then map the complicated return route. They are fond of diagrams and the enlightened teachers who explain them. Their sensitive spirits are grieved by having to live surrounded by common people with their sexual leers and stupid banana-peel jokes and vulgar groveling in the pigsty of animal appetite. Gnostics who go to church involuntarily pinch their noses on entering the pew, nervously apprehensive that an insensitive usher will seat a greasy sinner next to them. They are however enabled to endure by the considerable compensation of being "in the know" (gnostic means "the one who knows"). It is a good feeling to know that you are a cut above the common herd, superior to almost everyone you meet on the street or sit beside in church.

It is inevitable that gnostics will boycott the creation theater and avoid its language as much as possible, for metaphor is an affront to their gossamer immaterialities and inner-ring whispers, a loud fart in the salon of spirituality.

Metaphor is the psalmic antidote to the dematerializing venom of the gnostic. This language is so ruggedly and inescapably material. If we live in a country of shepherds, and know what it feels like to carry a shield, and have occasion from time to time to enter a fortress, and then address God as shepherd, and shield, and fortress, our metaphors bring us closer to the material world at the same time they bring us closer to God. When we pray we do not rise above the commonplaces of the material, but embrace them, and in embracing them find intimacy with the one who made them. Materiality is affirmed as precious.

And if we call God light, or rock, or mother (each a one-syllable word in Hebrew), we use ordinary language spoken and understood by any five year old. There is no chance of pretense in using these words, of pretending that our understanding of our relation to God depends on special insights or secret codes. Inner-ring secretiveness is exposed as nonsense. By using language in prayer that everyone else uses when they are not praying, we are kept in community with them. Nothing is more socializing than common speech; nothing more clique forming than jargon. The Psalms, by profuse and insistent use of metaphor, make it as difficult as they possibly can for us to sally off into vague abstractions, contemptuous of the actual grass under our feet, and call this verbal woolgathering prayer. They make it equally difficult for us to raise our noses in sophisticated superiority to the neighbors who breathe the same air we do, and suppose that is equivalent to raising our eyes to God in prayer simply because the angle of our heads is approximately the same.

The effects go the other way also: once we have used the word rock to address God, we are not likely to look on a rock the same way ever again, or a shepherd, or a mother. Metaphor notices, and then, pulled into prayer, sanctifies. Creation, entered into as into a theater in acts of prayer is seen (*theatros* means the place where we take a good look) with more attentiveness than otherwise, and then ceremoniously praised. When we use the same words in prayer that we use when working, traveling, fighting, eating, and drinking, the words become luminous and wondrous in prayer, and respect for these common actions is engendered in us.

Sacraments vs. Idols

Significantly, while the psalmists called God a rock, they never set up a rock and called it God. They called God a shepherd but never found a good-looking shepherd and made a statue of him to preserve the form of God. They called God a shield but never embellished one with precious stones, hung it in a sacred place, and worshiped it. The Hebrews who insisted strenuously on the holiness of matter and the divinity of creation—that the very ground was sacred!—were equally insistent that God was not matter and could not be represented by matter, even precious matter like silver and gold. They knew, by commandment and through the practice of prayer, the difference between an idol and a metaphor. An idol reduces and confines; a metaphor expands and connects. An idol starts with a mystery and fashions it into something that can be measured; a metaphor begins with something common and lets it expand into immeasurable glory. An idol gathers divinity into a lump—sometimes a very elegant and finely crafted lump, but a lump nevertheless—that can be controlled; a metaphor puts materiality into speech—the moment the word is spoken it is no longer under control, but is subject to the spontaneous dynamics of conversation in which a living God is partner.

The Psalms that teach us to pray by metaphor, using the experience of the senses to develop within us the experience of faith, come to fulfillment in Christ who was actual flesh and blood ("which we have seen with our eyes, which we have looked upon and touched with our hands," 1 John 1:1) thereby vindicating the goodness of the entire material creation. Jesus consistent with the diction of metaphor was also embarrassingly ordinary—"Is this not Joseph's son?" (Luke 4:22); "Why does your teacher eat with tax collectors and sinners?" (Matthew 9:11)—thereby slamming the door hard against all spiritual elitism. Jesus, in continuity with the Psalms, also taught us to pray in metaphor: "When you pray say, Father" (Luke 11:2).

The metaphors of the Psalms via the incarnation of Christ become a sacramental life, a life in which everything, every thing and person mediates God. Jesus was the master sacramentalist. He used anything at hand to bring us into an awareness of God and then into a response to God. The moment Jesus picked up something it was clear that it was not alien but belonging, a piece of God's creation that was a means for meeting God. Jugs of water at Cana, the sound of the wind in Jerusalem, Galilean sea waves, a paralytic's pallet at the Bethzathan pool, the corpse of Lazarus. Things. "There is no good trying to be more spiritual than God. God never meant man to be a purely spiritual creature. That is why He used material things like bread and wine to put new life into us. We may think this rather crude and unspiritual. God does not: He invented eating. He liked matter. He invented it."⁴

Baron Friedrich von Hügel never tired of saying that spirit and sense go together in Christian prayer.⁵ Whenever we look on creaturely beings within the world and consider them simply as they are and in depth, and pray what we see, we are carried by and through them to God by whom every creature exists and whom every creature makes manifest. Things cannot be bypassed. They are as essential in the prayer closet as in bed and board. Metaphor in prayer develops into sacramental living, gets rid of illusion and evasion so that we live and pray firsthandedly, seeing, smelling, touching and breathing the reality of our days, and then loving or hating it, blessing or cursing it, whatever we decide, but never indifferent to it, never insulated from it.

The Emphatic "Yes"

There are two great mystical traditions in the life of prayer, sometimes labeled apophatic and kataphatic. *Apophemi* is the Greek "no"; *kataphemi* is "yes." Apophatic prayer is nay saying, the *via negativa*. It shuts its eyes so as not to be distracted or diverted from the pure being of God. Kataphatic prayer is yea saying, the *via affirmativa*. It opens its eyes, letting lights and colors, icons and incense draw us into their, and our, source in God.

There is certainly a place for apophatic prayer: our imaginations are rampant with neurotic lust and escapist longings that get projected against a cosmic widescreen we ignorantly name God. Marvel and miracle, sensation and sentiment, doomsday fear and infantile eroticism are thrown together and made into what we suppose to be a god. Prayers are constantly being addressed out of and to such fantasies. Such prayers need fasting, and plenty of it, to purge them of their fantasies.

But kataphatic prayer is surely normative: the Psalms train us in it, the incarnation confirms it, and the sacraments perpetuate it. The rubric for apophatic prayer is, "fold your hands, bow your head, shut your eyes, and we'll pray." But the psalmists are kataphatic to a man, to a woman—they take us to the theater where we see "mountains skip like rams" (Ps. 114:4) and hear "trees clap their hands" (Isa. 55:12); they show us how to pray with our eyes open, wide open.

I will tell of thy name to my brethen;
in the midst of the congregation I will praise thee.

PSALM 22:22

Where two or three are gathered in my name, there am I in the
midst of them.

ST. MATTHEW 18:20

The liturgy that afternoon penetrated the secret channels of
his brain; he understood his mouth's work for the first time,
even though he had chanted those same words every day from
boyhood, and they were as familiar to him as his own
bedclothes. These domesticated and intimate syllables had all
at once taken on an enchantment, an illumination. He was
stunned by what he heard in them. He left the prayer hall
exulting, strange even to himself.

CYNTHIA OZICK

7. Liturgy

When we go to prayer in the Psalms we find, often to our surprise, that we have been ushered to a pew in the vigorously rich worship of Israel. When David organized Israel into a worshiping congregation, thirty-eight thousand Levites were assigned to provide the leadership and support required (1 Chron. 23:3). Prayer in Israel was not left up to individuals to do or not do as they more or less felt inclined. This was a public works project of impressive dimensions. It was neither private nor peripheral. Common worship takes precedence over private devotions.

Selah, scattered randomly through the Psalms seventy-one times, is the evidence. The word never occurs within the text itself but alongside as a notation in the margin. No one is sure of its exact meaning; scholars guess "pause for a benediction" perhaps, or "louder here—*fortissimo!* "[1] What is beyond guesswork is that it is telltale evidence of liturgy. Like detectives sifting through clues we find *Selah*; from it we deduce not a crime but a community. People were gathered together in prayer by and in these psalms. Congregations were assembled in worship. These prayers are not from the pen of solitary mystics; these are the trained voices of choirs lifting their voices in lament and praise, in petition and adoration.

These psalms that teach us to pray are, all of them, prayers of people gathered as a community before God in worship. Some of them most certainly originated in solitude, and all of them have been continued in solitude. But in the form in which they come to us, the *only* form in which they come to us, and therefore in the way they serve as our school of prayer, they are the prayers of the community before God in worship. Prayer is fundamentally liturgical. *Selah*, untranslated and untranslatable, strewn through the Psalms, will not let us forget it. If its *meaning* is an enigma, its use is clear: *Selah* directed people who were *together* in prayer to do something or other *together*. Our prayer book, by the time we get our hands on it, has all these liturgical scribbles in the margins. Biblically, we are not provided with a single prayer for private devotions. The community in prayer, not the individual at prayer, is basic and primary. The Americanization of prayer has reversed this clear biblical (and human!) order. Individuals don't "make up" the community, they are produced by it. The Psalms return us to this beginning, this original matrix of humanity and spirituality.[2]

Prayer requires community. Prayer is not possible outside of, apart from, or in spite of the praying community. God calls to his people to come before him and hear his word, to obey his commands and receive his blessings. We hear the call and come. We bow our heads and close our eyes. We pray. We open our eyes, look around and see, sometimes to our great surprise, that others are there also. Helmer Ringgren told us bluntly: "The Psalms were not written for private use."[3] We were not invited, it seems, to a private audience with our God.

The assumption that prayer is what we do when we are alone—the solitary soul before God—is an egregious, and distressingly persistent, error. We imagine a lonely shepherd on the hills composing lyrics to the glory of God. We imagine a beleaguered soul sinking in a swamp of trouble calling for help. But our imaginations betray us. We are part of something before we are anything, and never more so than when we pray. Prayer begins in community.

The Courtesy of Liturgy

Liturgy is not, as some suppose, aesthetics. It is courtesy. And theology. It is being mindful that there are others to whom God speaks and who risk their lives in an answer. It is the gracious acknowledgment that others in the family also have needs and rights, and that I am neither the only nor the favorite child.

Liturgy clears a space for meeting, appoints a time, and provides an order. Prayer takes place in space and time; we are not angels. Prayer takes place with people; we are not monads. Liturgy can be elaborate or simple, baroque or bare, but it always provides for these three things: space, time, order. We know next to nothing about the liturgy of Israel, and not much more about the early church, but that does not matter; we do not pray by archeology.[4] The important thing is that *there was* a liturgy, and we know that beyond cavil. People came together at appointed times in agreed upon places and used psalms to pray—this most personal and individual of all acts!—as a community. Jesus confirmed the basic liturgical character of prayer when he said, "Where two or three are gathered in my name there am I in the midst of them" (Matt. 18:20).

God is one but his people are many. He has a single purpose for us, but we are a motley congeries of temperament, need, and understanding. When we pray we become more deeply aware than ever of our irreplaceable uniqueness; but we also pray to the God who wills his common love to be exchanged among us. How can our fundamental unity before the one God in our prayer be nurtured and deepened and not torn into a thousand sects? How can we become more ourselves than ever without becoming more selfish than ever? How can we prevent Corinthian anarchy, one of the commonest and most troubling side effects of prayer? Israel's answer, on display in the Psalms and embraced by the church, is "liturgy."

The Unselfing of Prayer

"To the choirmaster," a second liturgical notation, is inserted as a heading in fifty-five psalms. The word *m'natseah* is not in itself a liturgical word. When the temple was being built or repaired, a director *(m'natseah)* was on hand to provide oversight, coordinating the work. When the temple was being used as a house of prayer, there was also a director *(m'natseah)* to give leadership. The frequency of the word as a heading to the Psalms shows that a director was commonly involved in the praying life of Israel: someone was assigned to lead them in prayer. Praying in a church is no more a private enterprise than building a church.

The implications of this are far-reaching and profound for all who learn to pray: we learn to pray by being led in prayer. We commonly think of prayer as what we do out of our own needs and on our own initiative. We experience a deep longing for God, and so we pray. We feel an artesian gush of gratitude to God, and so we pray. We are crushed with a truckload of guilt before God, and so we pray. But in a liturgy we do not take the initiative; it is not our experience that precipitates prayer. Someone stands in front of us and says, "Let us pray." We don't start it; someone else starts it, and we fall into step behind or alongside. Our egos are no longer front and center.

This is so important, for prayer by its very nature is answering speech. The consensus of the entire Christian community upholds the primacy of God's word in everything: in creation, in salvation, in judgment, in blessing, in mercy, and in grace. But in the practice of prayer, inebriated as we often are by our own heady subjectivity, we boozily set aside the primacy of God's word and substitute the primacy of our words. We are so sure that here, at least, we get the first word!

But when we take our place in a worshiping congregation we are not in charge. Someone else has built the place of prayer; someone else has established the time for prayer; someone else tells us to begin to pray. All of this takes place in a context in which the word of God is primary: God's word audible in scripture and sermon, God's word visible in baptism and eucharist. This is the center in which we learn to pray. We do not, of course, remain in this center: lines of praying radiate and lead us outwards. From this center we go to our closets or the mountains, into the streets and the markets, and continue our praying. But it is essential to understand that the prayer goes from the center *outwards;* if we suppose that it proceeds inwards from the convergence of praying individuals we are at cross-purposes with the praying experience of Israel and the church.

The benefit that flows from this is enormous. It more than compensates for the painful (at least it seems so) sacrifice of initiative: we are rescued from the tyranny of our feelings.

Feelings are the scourge of prayer. To pray by feelings is to be at the mercy of glands and weather and digestion. And there is no mercy in any of them. Feelings lie. Feelings deceive. Feelings seduce. Because they are so emphatically *there*, and so incontrovertibly *interior*, it is almost inevitable that we take our feelings seriously as reputable guides to the reality that is deep within us—our hearts before God.

But feelings are no more spiritual than muscles. They are entirely physical. They are real, and they are important. But they are real and important in the same way that our fingernails and noses are important—we would not want to live without them (although we could if we had to), but their length and shape and color tell us nothing about our life with God. To suppose that our emotions in any way give us reliable evidence of the nature or quality of our life with God is to misinterpret them. They are wonderful and necessary and glorious. They are part of the rich and stunning complexity of the human being in the image of God. We must value and develop and share them. But they are not prayer. All the spiritual masters are careful to guide us in a detachment from our feelings as a means for discerning grace or guiding prayer. St. John of the Cross, as passionate and earthy a man as ever lived, had little patience with people who indulged their "spiritual sweet tooth" and then lapsed into "spiritual gluttony."[5]

But how do we both affirm our feelings and detach ourselves from them? Through liturgy. We pray not when we feel like it but when someone, the pastor, the priest, the "choirmaster"! says, "Let us pray." We lose nothing of our emotions except their tyranny. The gamut of emotions experienced in our human condition is given full expression in the Psalms. We pray through each psalm and hit every note, sound every tone of feeling that we are capable of and learn to be at home with all of them before God. But the feelings do not have the first and controlling word.

God does. The feelings are incorporated in the prayers, not the prayers in the feelings. Liturgical prayer misses not a single heartbeat of our emotions, but refuses even a hint of direction from them.

If we insist on maintaining the initiative in prayer, praying when we feel like it according to what we feel we need, we take on a psychic burden that is too much for us. Finally we slump to the ground in exhaustion and give it all up. After a few hours or days or weeks, usually out of guilt, we get up again and give it another try. That is why there is so much intermittent prayer—people who pray in spurts and then lapse, leaving behind them abandoned schemes, failed methods, but always on the lookout for another that will keep them faithful in prayer. It never occurs to them to let the "choirmaster " do that part for them. If we insist on conducting our lives of prayer as a private enterprise, we take on a monumental task that we have no adequate means for carrying out. But the liturgy provides an adequate means. Liturgy depsychologizes prayer. It removes prayer from the control of my emotions, my motivations, my physical energy, and my circumstances.

Recovery of Community

The third liturgical direction in the Psalms is musical. Twenty-nine times either an instrumental accompaniment or a tune is assigned to a prayer: "with stringed instruments" in Psalm 4 and "for the flutes" in Psalm 5 are examples of the former; "according to the Gittith" of Psalm 8 and "according to Muth-labben" of Psalm 9 are examples of the latter. These directions show that the Hebrews did a lot of singing (or chanting) when they prayed.

Song brings our prayers into rhythm and harmony with the other members of the community. We are never more ourselves than when we pray, but if we remain only ourselves, we are less than ourselves. Liturgy installs us praying in a community. We don't, of course, know everyone in the community. We don't know what they are experiencing at any given moment. We don't know what temptations and trials, what joys and blessings, what ecstasy and grace, what boredom and sin are under the surface demeanor of those whom we meet. But it is God's will that none of us do any of this alone. How can we pray accurately for and harmoniously with the other members of God's people? Through song: song establishes all the members of the congregation in organic relationship. The Christian recovers a sense of community and experiences the dynamics of community not through the categories of sociology but through the music of liturgy.

We would prefer to stand tall and alone in our prayers. But our stature and individuality are never the most important thing in prayer: God *is;* our neighbors are *there.* We live before God, in community. Liturgical prayer, by means of tunes and instruments, trains us in this mature awareness and participation, and at the same time protects us from the subjective and the sentimental.

Music pulls us into coordinated participation with people whose voices are very different from ours without in any way reducing or blurring the distinctiveness of each voice. The way of music is not to get everyone together "in one heart and mind" by assigning a single tone, say an F sharp, which is then practiced until all can intone it identically. The way of music is to pull together all the different timbres and qualities of voice, and weave them into rich harmonies, preserving the uniqueness of each one.

I open the Psalms at random, and find myself in the place of prayer, ready to pray. I look around and see thirty other men and women. Some of them I recognize, most I do not. They have come from thirty different places, were reared in thirty different homes, and in the past few hours have experienced thirty different combinations of emotions. Some come from a brutalizing experience, some from a birthday celebration, some are full of hate at what has been done to them, others brimming with joy over the incredible beauties of the day. By means of creation and covenant I know that I am one with these people, but I don't feel at one with them or in common with them. How can I? We are all so different, and the deeper anyone probes within us the more different we will each be found to be. How can I enter into and develop the single love that God has for us all? The leader announces Psalm 56 to be sung to the tune "The Dove on Far-off Terebinths." The prayer seethes with experiences of brutality and hate. Hate is the most remote thing from my life right now, but within moments I am praying the experience of hate, in tune with others who may or may not be experiencing it. Brutality is the most remote thing from my life this moment, but as the prayer progresses I am praying the experience of brutality, in tune with others who may or may not be experiencing it. I feel surrounded by friends, but in prayer I enter into common cause with persons who are desperately facing enemies. As I continue to pray the Psalms seriatim, i.e., in a series, which is the oldest practice of the praying community, I will pray all the experiences of the community both local and worldwide—the African community, the Russian community, the Guatemalan community. I am steadily and surely integrated into the community of the oppressed and blessed. I am pulled out of prayer that is self-oriented and self-indulgent. I am given adequate means for intercession and celebration, neither of which is a private act.

I will, most certainly, continue to pray when I am by myself behind the shut door of my closet. I will never postpone praying until the scheduled hour of worship has arrived. I do not wait for a liturgical quorum to give validity to my prayer. Prayer takes place in every detail of life, in the loneliest reaches of our hearts and the most isolated of exiles, whether geographical or emotional. There is much silence to be cultivated, and great stretches of solitude to be guarded, for these, silence and solitude, are as essential to the soul as meat and potatoes are to the body. But all the same, just as the basic form of humanity is community so the basic form of prayer is liturgical: the structure in which we learn to pray is the assembled and ordered community before God.[6]

Even when we pray the Psalms by ourselves (which most people will do most of the time), we are not by ourselves: community is always implicit in the Psalms and the moment we pray them we are drawn into the community. David danced these psalms before the ark and the Hebrews in Solomon's Temple chanted them. Children running down the slope of Olivet waved palm branches and shouted these psalms and Jesus in the upper room with his disciples sang them. The Corinthian Christians celebrated the eucharist with these psalms and the apocalyptic 144,000 fill heaven with them.

We need not fear the impersonal and the procrustean in the liturgical. A choir is not a committee. Liturgy does not homogenize praying people who pray into a pious porridge; colors, sounds, and movements are sharpened; precise relationships and coordinates are etched. There is nothing in the Psalms to indicate that their liturgical use ever leveled anyone down to a lowest "crowd" denominator. Sharp-edged and angular individuality is one of the most marked characteristics of the Psalms. Only a deficient sense of community misleads us into interpreting the intense and intimate individuality of the Psalms as the product of private experience. We are most ourselves when we are in relationships of grace and love; the relationships that are paradigmatic for our healed and holy lives are most evident in common worship.

Liturgical Defenses

Left to ourselves, we are never more selfish than when we pray. With God as the Great Sympathizer, the Great Giver, the Great Promiser we go to our knees and indulge every impulse for gratification. But the Psalms that teach us to pray never leave us to ourselves; they embed all our prayers in liturgy. Liturgy defends us against the commonest diseases of prayer: the tyranny of our emotions, the isolationism of our pride.

Liturgy pulls our prayers out of the tiresome business of looking after ourselves and into the exhilarating enterprise of seeing and participating in what God is doing. We are drawn into a large generosity where everyone is getting and receiving, offering and praising. We are drawn to the place where people are being loved and where they love us. We are deepened into the practice of humanity in covenant with God that goes both beneath and beyond our self-defined religious desire. We are put beside people who help us and whom we can help. Liturgy breaks us out of the isolation of ego and emotion where we are cut off from the large winds and landscapes of grace. God wants us outside the walls that quarantine us in our ego-sickness; he pulls us into the great dance of grace in which we find ourselves moving rhythmically and joyfully with partner after partner. *Selah*—indeed!

All day long they seek to injure my cause;
    all their thoughts are against me for evil.
They band themselves together, they lurk,
    they watch my steps.
As they have waited for my life,
    so recompense them for their crime;
    in wrath cast down the peoples, O God!

PSALMS 56:5-7

And lead us not into temptation, but deliver us from evil.

JESUS (MATTHEW 6:13)

I think that taking life seriously means something such as this;
that whatever man does on this planet has to be done in the
lived truth of the terror of creation, of the grotesque, of the
rumble of panic underneath everything. Otherwise it is false.

ERNEST BECKER

8. Enemies

There is a pseudo-prayer that promises its practitioners entrance into the subliminal harmonies of the way-things-are, putting them in tune with the general hum of the universe. This so-called prayer reduces tension, lowers stress, and extends longevity. The people who get good at it are calm, their voices soothing, and their actions poised. They meditate beautiful thoughts and sleep well. They cultivate the way of peace.

Psalm-prayer also enters into the way-things-are, but finds that the way-things-are is pretty bad. Evil is encountered. Wickedness is confronted. This prayer quickens the pulse and shoots adrenalin into the bloodstream. The people who practice this prayer get excited—they yell and gesture. They are engaged, or soon to be engaged, in an act of war. Prayer is combat. Prayer brings us before God—and there, before God, we find ourselves grappling with "the world rulers of this present darkness, against the spiritual hosts of wickedness in the heavenly places" (Ephesians 6:12).

There are harmonies to be experienced in prayer, but they are all achieved harmonies, not natural ones. They are hard-won in Genesis creations, Peniel wrestlings, and Gethsemane struggles. If there are surface calms in our lives and in society, and there often are for some, a dive beneath the surface shows forces locked in combat.

People who are looking for a spiritual soporific don't pray the Psalms, or at least don't pray them for very long. The Psalms are full of unsettling enemy talk. God is the primary subject in the Psalms, but enemies are established in solid second place. Why should this be? How does it happen that in the very place we find the most intense concern for God and the most developed converse with him that is imaginable, right alongside without buffer or warning, there is this inordinate preoccupation with enemies? Shouldn't an overpowering sense of God's presence, his power and salvation, shrink human difficulties into insignificance? And shouldn't an immersion in the great realities of mercy transform every retaliatory impulse into an evangel that makes us "love everybody" as the old-time religion does for country singers?

It is not unreasonable to suppose that the life of prayer will draw us into a genial camaraderie, so secure in God's grace and confident in his beneficence that we are irresistibly carried along in the flow of the river of God, viewing everyone and everything with the cheeriest of feelings. But reason, at least reason inexperienced and untested in the life of prayer, isn't the best guide in these matters. When we take the Psalms as our guide, we find that people who pray have a lot of enemies, and that they spend a lot of their praying time dealing with them.

Most of us would prefer it otherwise. We commonly indulge our preference by subjecting the Psalms to severe editing, cutting away any negativism that offends piety and disturbs the peace. The editing is usually unconscious, accomplished by the simple expedient of withdrawing the imagination and sliding over the offensive passages.[1] Psalm 137 is on nearly everyone's list for revision. Psalm 137 is the scandal of the Psalter.

The Scandal Psalm

Psalm 137 was first prayed out of Israel's painful exile. There are three stanzas. The first two stanzas are poignant: these lyrics draw us into creative and mysterious depths where a human being in the very act of being humiliated is ennobled, in the course of being violated is exalted.

"By the waters of Babylon, there we sat down and wept" opens the first stanza. In the loneliness of exile, the Israelites with their far-flung reputation for robust song and hearty praise are grist for Babylonia taunts: "Sing us one of your Zion songs!" But all the music has been knocked out of them. Their lives and voices are flat as the desert plain of their exile.

Stanza two deepens the sorrow: "How shall I sing the Lord's song in a foreign land?" Silence is their only dignity. To sing in this place, among these people, would be a sacrilege. They will be loyal to their homeland and honor the memories of their grand and holy place of worship in reverberating silence.

In these two stanzas, the fine-tempered steel forged in the exile sufferings of loss, rejection, and violation is fashioned into sharp images and penetrating rhythms that cut to the center of our hearts and make us companions in their weeping prayer and silent pain. Their pathos and art bring us to our knees in prayer with and for them. Then there is this:

> Remember, O Lord, against the Edomites
>   the day of Jerusalem.
> how they said, "Rase it, rase it!
>   Down to its foundations!"
> O daughter of Babylon, you devastator!
>   Happy shall he be who requites you
>   with what you have done to us!
> Happy shall he be who takes your little ones
>   and dashes them against the rocks!

Psalms 1 and 2, set as an introduction to the Psalms in order to draw us into the way of prayer, began and ended with the word blessed, or happy (ashrey). Psalm 1 directed us to the practice of torah-meditation, giving our full attention to the word that God speaks to us so that in prayer we will not be distracted by what everyone else is talking about, but attentive in answering the God who is talking to us. Persons who do this meditative listening and answering are called blessed. Psalm 2 directs us to the practice of messiah-expectation, paying attention to the way God enters into history in human form and establishes his rule so that we will not be intimidated by the bully bravado of unbelieving rulers. Persons who trust in this messianic presence are called blessed.

Psalm 137 uses this same word—blessed, happy (ashrey)— twice in its climax lines. It uses it in the contextual way that has been firmly established through torah-meditation and messiah-expectation, but it is now put to the service of enemy-denunciation: "Happy shall he be who takes your little ones and dashes them against the rocks!"

This is raw hate. Nothing in the preceding lines of Psalm 137 has prepared us for this. This is a can of black spray paint defacing a memorial in white marble. Who let this in our prayer book? And hadn't we better get it out? A lot of people think so. In edition after edition of prayer books, hymnbooks, and worship books that are based on the Psalms, we find this stanza excised. These psalmectomies are well intentioned, no doubt, but wrongheaded all the same.

They are wrongheaded because our hate needs to be prayed, not suppressed. Hate is our emotional link with the spirituality of evil. It is the volcanic eruption of outrage when the holiness of being, ours or another's, has been violated. It is also the ugliest and most dangerous of our emotions, the hair trigger on a loaded gun. Embarrassed by the ugliness and fearful of the murderous, we commonly neither admit or pray our hate; we deny it and suppress it. But if it is not admitted it can quickly and easily metamorphose into the evil that provokes it; and if it is not prayed we have lost an essential insight and energy in doing battle with evil.

Dishonesty in prayer is already rampant enough without an assist from bleeding heart editors. The Hebrew editors who selected the psalms for our praying were a tougher breed; they included the third stanza of Psalm 137 deliberately and with good reason: the life of prayer carries us into difficult country, a country in which we become aware that evil is far more extensive than anything we ever guessed, where malignity has worked itself perversely and deeply into the world's ways. As Kant said, "Evil is radical." We didn't know things were this bad. Neither our minds or our emotions are prepared to deal with this. We thrash about. We sputter in outrage. We curse the so recently identified enemy. We demand vengeance.

We have been brought up, most of us, interpreting what is

wrong in the world on a grid of moralism. Moralism trains us in making cool, detached judgments. Deep down, the moralist suspects that there are no, or at least not very many, real victims. People get what is coming to them. In the long run people reap what they sow. The rape victim, the unemployed, the emotionally ill, the prisoner, the refugee—if we were privy to all the details we would see that, in fact, "they asked for it."

The Psalms will have none of this. The Psalms assume a moral structure to life, but their main work is not to train us in judgmental moralism but to grapple with evil. Their praying insights have identified an enemy and they respond in outrage. They hate what they see. On behalf of all the dispossessed, the mocked, the dehumanized of the earth they pour into the ears of God their sightings of the enemy, not "siphoning off hate, but channeling it in effective ways, in covenantal shapes."[2]

This hate arises in a context of holiness: meditating on the holy word of God, expecting the holy messiah of God. Before we prayed we would sit peacefully for two or three hours reading about suffering and cruelty as if we were reading about long-extinct dinosaurs, a knowledgeable but detached acquaintance. But immersed by prayer in this holiness, we see clearly what we never saw before, the utter and terrible sacrilege of enemies who violate a good creation, who brutalize women and men who are made, every one them in the image of God. There is an enormous amount of suffering epidemic in the world because of evil people. The rape and pillage are so well concealed in polite language and courteous conventions that some people can go years without seeing it. And we ourselves did not see it. But now we see it. And we hate it. We are ejected from our cushioned private religion into solidarity with "the Silent Servants of the Used, Abused and Utterly Screwed up."[3]

Just as hurt is the usual human experience that brings us to our knees praying for help, provoking the realization that we need God, so hate is frequently the human experience that brings us to our feet praying for justice, catalyzing our concern for the terrible violations against life all around us. Hate is often the first sign that we care. If we are far gone in complacency, it is often the only emotion with enough velocity to penetrate our protective sumgness and draw red blood. That does not mean that prayer legitimizes hate—it uses it. "Surely the wrath of men shall praise thee" (Psalm 76:10). Neither is hurt good, but it wakes us to our need for help. Human hurt is not a very promising first step to the accomplishment of wholeness; human hate is not a very promising first step to the establishment of righteousness. Nevertheless, when prayed, they are steps, first steps into the presence of God where we learn that he has ways of dealing with what we bring him that are both other and better than what we had in mind. But until we are in prayer, we are not teachable. It is better to pray badly than not to pray at all. A ship that is dead in the water can't be steered.

We want to be at our best before God. Prayer, we think, means presenting ourselves before God so that he will be pleased with us. We put on our Sunday best in our prayers. Psalm 137 is well on the way of doing just what we expect, bringing out the best in us when, without warning, this fissure opens up—a dark crevasse of hate—and brings out the worst.

It is easy to be honest before God with our hallelujahs; it is somewhat more difficult to be honest in our hurts; it is nearly impossible to be honest before God in the dark emotions of our hate. So we commonly suppress our negative emotions (unless, neurotically, we advertise them). Or, when we do express them, we do it far from the presence, or what we think is the presence, of God, ashamed or embarrassed to be seen in these curse-stained bib overalls. But when we pray the psalms, these classic prayers of God's people, we find that will not do. We must pray who we actually are, not who we think we should be. In prayer, all is not sweetness and light. The way of prayer is not to cover our unlovely emotions so that they will appear respectable, but expose them so that they can be enlisted in the work of the kingdom. "It is an act of profound faith to entrust one's most precious hatreds to God, knowing they will be taken seriously."[4]

Hate, prayed, takes our lives to bedrock where the foundations of justice are being laid.

The Angry Psalmists

Psalm 137 is the most celebrated outbreak of hate in the Psalms (and the most tampered with) but by no means an exception. There is hardly a page of the Psalms that isn't left smoking by a pungent curse.

> Break thou the arm of the wicked and evildoer. (10:15)
> On the wicked he will rain coals of fire and brimstone. (11:16)
> May their belly be filled with what thou hast stored up for them. (17:14)
> You will aim at their faces with your bows. (21:121)
> God will scatter the bones of the ungodly (53.5)
> O God, break the teeth in their mouths. (58:6)
> Let them be blotted out of the book of the living. (69:28)
> Terrify them with thy hurricane! (83:15)
> He clothed himself with cursing as his coat, may it soak into his body like water, like oil into his bones! (109:18)
> He will execute judgment among the nations, filling them with corpses. (110:6)
> O that thou wouldst slay the wicked, O God. . . . I hate them with perfect hatred. (139:22)

The psalmists are angry people. In the presence of God they have realized that the world is not a benign place where everyone is doing their best to get along with the others and that if we all just try a little harder things are going to turn out all right. Their prayers have brought them to an awareness in their souls and in society of the prophesied consequences of the "enmity between you [Satan] and the woman" (Gen. 3:15).

We are easily duped by evil. Evil almost never looks like an enemy in its presenting forms. There was nothing in the wilderness temptations of Jesus to indicate that anything evil was involved—provide bread for hunger, furnish a miracle to encourage belief, acquire power that could be used to establish a just world society. But Jesus had been in prayer for forty days and nights and saw through the polite and plausible offers. His prayers had given him discernment. He identified the options as enemies. When he emerged from the wilderness it was not to negotiate in sweet reasonableness but to do battle: "I have come to cast fire on the earth" (Luke 12:49).

The last book of the bible, the Revelation to St. John, is frequently indicted for its violent language and vindictive spirit against the wicked. But St. John learned it all in the school of the Psalms, and from Jesus who was also, as the mountain people say, a good cusser. Jesus called Peter the very devil, the Pharisees vipers on their way to hell, and shouted down woes on the heads of those who used religion as a way to make themselves comfortable at the terrible cost of oppressing the weak and exploiting the poor (Matt. 16:23, Matthew 23). As the end approached Jesus took the cruelest verb in Psalm 137 and used it against Babylon, alias Jerusalem, as the enemies of God prepared to murder the messiah of God.[5]

Love Your Enemies

The last word on the enemies is with Jesus, who captured the Psalms:[6] "Love your enemies and pray for them that persecute you." But loving enemies presupposes that we know that they are there, whether many or few, and have begun to identify them. Enemies, especially for those who live by faith, are a fact of life. If we don't know we have them or who they are, we live in a dangerous naïveté, unguarded from the "pestilence that stalks in darkness" and "the destruction that wastes at noonday," witless when we pray "deliver us from evil."

Our hate is used by God to bring the enemies of life and salvation to notice, and then involve us in active compassion for the victims. Once involved we find that while hate provides the necessary spark for ignition, it is the wrong fuel for the engines of judgment; only love is adequate to sustain these passions.

But we must not imagine that loving and praying for our enemies in love is a strategy that will turn them into good friends. Love is the last thing that our enemies want from us and often acts as a goad to redoubled fury. Love requires vulnerability, forgiveness, and response; the enemies want power and control and dominion. The enemies that Jesus loved and prayed for killed him.

I will call to mind the deeds of the Lord;
  yea, I will remember thy wonders of old.
I will meditate on all thy work,
  and muse on thy mighty deeds.
Thy way, O God, is holy.
  What god is great like our God?

PSALM 77:11–13

Do this in remembrance of me.

JESUS (1 CORINTHIANS 11:24)

Our planet that gets smaller every year, with its fantastic
proliferation of mass media, is witnessing a process that
escapes definition, characterized by a refusal to remember.
The poet feels anxiety, for he senses in this a foreboding of a
not distant future when history will be reduced to what
appears on television, while the truth, because it is too
complicated, will be buried in the archives, if not totally
annihilated.

CZESLAW MILOSZ

9. Memory

Prayer begins as the most spontaneous of acts: pain, gratitude, anger. It occurs in fragments. It is experienced abruptly without transitions. But as it continues, it develops subterranean connections—gathering and arranging—and becomes our most comprehensive action. Prayer matures into the practice of memory.

It is common among those who teach us the Psalms to arrange them by style or type: thanksgiving psalms, nature psalms, messianic psalms, forgiveness psalms. This is well intentioned but misguided. Prayer does not tidy up the dishabille of our everydayness. Prayer does not arrange our disordered lives into labeled file folders. Prayer is the intensification of life. Since life does not come to us in neat categories, neither does prayer. The Psalms teach us to pray by immersing us in the stream of life as it comes to us, wet and wild.

There is considerable evidence of editorial activity in the Psalms but no evidence whatever of an attempt to arrange the psalms in categories of experience. Psalms of lament are not grouped together for our reference, followed, say, by psalms of thanksgiving. Such arrangements are useful for professors and their students, but the Psalms are not a textbook in which we study how others have prayed but a school in which we ourselves learn to pray. In the lives we actually live and in which the Psalms teach us to pray, experiences of lament are not organized into the first week of each month, followed the second week by experiences of thanksgiving. Experience arrives randomly. Jack-grief and Jill-pain tumble over one another down the same hillside. Doubt and faith are in a wrestling match, first one on top and then the other, in shifting supremacies.[1] We cannot order our lives into discrete categories; life comes—in Hopkins's adjectives, "dapple, fickle, freckled."[2]

We learn to pray not with a grammar, but with parents. The same way we learn language. Our first professors of English, our parents, do not first teach us nouns, then verbs, and follow these up with training in adjectives and adverbs, after which we learn imperatives and subjunctives. We get language as it comes to us, a tumble and tangle of words. We swim out of the silent womb into a noisy cataract, all the parts of speech crashing noisily into our ears in seeming disorder. Gradually morphemes find an ordered place in our mind and phonemes a coherent reproduction in our larynx and lips.

The Psalms are our parents, not our professors, in prayer. The grammatical sorting out of language into parts of speech has its place, but not when we are learning our cradle language. And the arrangement of psalms into forms also has its most useful place, but not as we are learning to pray our "mother tongue." We do better to simply enter the sequence of psalms as they are given to us in the Psalms, go from one to the next, one day to the next, one week to the next, taking what comes, learning to enter into what comes, whatever, practicing a sense of the presence of God, deepening that awareness into colloquy with God.

Along the way in doing this we acquire a sense of syntax. Words used in prayer (as in language itself) are not random sounds, however randomly they occur; an underlying syntax holds all words, spoken and prayed, in deep interconnection. Our prayers are infused with a sense of grammar. Praying the Psalms we deepen, sharpen and extend our memories so that we have ready access to all the parts of speech—parts of experience!—that are available to creatures who live on this "third planet from the sun."[3]

That we should be able to remember—recall and reassemble all the fragments of emotions and ideas, sights and sounds, people with whom we talked and books that we have read and pull them into this present moment—is a staggering achievement. Memory, by which "bits of visual, verbal and emotional glass are embedded in the mosaic I come to know as me is certainly the brain's most essential function."[4]

We live, necessarily, in the present tense, but most of what we live with is from the past tense, inherited from our ancestors, acquired through our genes, reported to us by our senses, given by others in food, guidance, and knowledge. If we are alienated from this massive foundation that is the ocean floor of our existence, we exist meagerly on the thin edge of the present without depth and without wisdom.

There are three large areas in this recovery and practice of memory in prayer: we recover a sense of the shape of creation in us, we recover a realization of the many ways in which we are implicated in sin; we recover a feel for the country of salvation. But the working of the memory in prayer is not simply a recollection of facts so that we can pass examinations. What takes place is that what has happened to us, in us and around us—the facts that stream into us through our genes and our culture and our meetings—are metabolized into daily life. Prayer takes our genetic, cultural, and social experience and gets it circulating in our bloodstream as faith and hope and love, building muscles, lubricating our elbows and knees, replacing dead skin with fresh, repairing lesions.

The Shape of Creation

Prayer recovers the shape of our creation. We are created in "the image of God." We are declared, on the authority of Genesis, "good." We, and everyone and everything around us has this basic beauty, this wondrous goodness. But we very often don't feel at all good. We do not perceive ourselves "in the image of God." We are conscious of failure and inadequacy; we experience criticism and rejection; we feel lousy. The memory of our good creation is obscured in a thick fog of failure and inadequacy.

Prayer is a reentry into the reality of our good creation. The Psalms, all spoken out of this ordered and purposed beauty, activate our memories of creation. Always, this Genesis milieu is implicit; sometimes it is explicit. When we pray the Psalms we consciously enter the reality of our good creation.

Our lives are bracketed by God: "O Lord, our Lord, how majestic is thy name in all the earth!" is the first and last line of both Psalm 8 and of our lives. Within the brackets—and there is nothing that is not within the brackets—our creation takes place. We very often lose a sense of boundary, of limit, of orientation. We feel "lost in the cosmos."[5] The extreme form of this alienation is found in the schizophrenic, the person who is not sure where his or her personality ends and another's begins, and who therefore lives in a terrifying inner disorder, a dizzying loss of definition. A developed sense of creation, of being created, is at the same time a sense of definition—lines of distinction are clear between me and you, between me and the animals, between me and the trees and stars and sea. Most of all between me and God. It is the delineation of God as Creator and myself as creature that allows me to perceive the forms of beauty in which I am an active participant.

The verbal act of naming God begins the recovery of order. Saying the name God in itself restores orientation. When I name the Name, I have a grip on a rope by which I can be pulled from the mire of subjectivism: my life is now oriented to another who is more and other than I am. Every act of addressing another by name is a declaration of the reality of creation: I am distinct from the one I am naming, therefore I am a creature, therefore there is a Creator. The Psalms are resplendent with names for God and the naming of God. Invocations are legion. God is addressed by a variety of names and metaphors (Lord, Most High, Almighty, Rock, Shield) and in a wide ranging expression of moods and intensities (hear me, incline thine ear, attend to my cry, draw near to my groaning, listen to my prayer).

Also, the continuation of speech after the personal address is an assertion of created order. No matter how disordered our speech, no matter how disoriented our experience, the act of putting it into words puts it into form: order is worked back into our systems in the very act of praying our formlessness, our ugliness, our chaos. The act of speech brings us into order, one word after another, one sentence after another.

There is more: the Psalms are poetry, which means that the order of the words is even more deliberate than in prose. There are repetitions and proportions, sound patterns and intricate plays of meaning set in dancing rhythms. Formlessness takes form. The poetic mind, which is a creative mind following creative patterns after the manner of its Creator, begins to display the forms of creation in the very speech that questions whether there is anything remotely resembling creation. The psalmist blubbers,

> I am weary with my moaning
> Every night I flood my bed with tears
> I drench my couch with my weeping. (Psalm 6:6)

The sogginess of tear-drenched bed clothes and a swampy mattress becomes crisp and clean edged by means of metaphor and rhythm. Formlessness takes form. Creation is experienced: a creation embedded in the person by virtue of simply being here now emerges into consciousness in the act of speech.

The recovery of the shape of our creation does not come by arranging our lives in neat categories but in the recovery of language in acts of prayer. Prayer does not (or at least in this area it does not) bring something new to us, but brings into expression what is there, activating memory so that we have before us, in fact, what we experience many times as language users: we say a word and it becomes a sentence; the words call attention to the shape of a star, the presence of a tree, the movement of a lion; we recognize the reality of another; we are faced with the incontrovertible evidence of a piece of history—a journey, a meal, a camping place. Things happen: the succession of days does not obliterate them. Objects are there, holding together in a molecular stability. Persons exist with recognizable identities whether they are laughing or crying, rich or poor. In the act of praying the Psalms the faded memory of our creation is brought into experienced clarity.

Our Implication in Sin

We also recover our sense of implication in sin. If the deeply embedded memory of our good creation is frequently and easily lost to our consciousness, the realization that we are implicated in a catastrophic sin is just as frequently lost. We pretend that we are better than we are. We deny the evidence of our wrongdoing. We avoid facing our badness. But every avoidance or denial of sin is no less an escape from our humanity than the avoidance and denial of our creation. For sin also is the reality of our lives, and coexists alongside the creation, interpenetrating in a most confusing way.

The Psalms pray us into a detailed awareness of our condition as sinners. The memory of our good creation depends upon maintaining a lively sense of God in our lives (which is what prayer, more than anything else, gives us); the awareness of our sin also requires a lively sense of a living God.

The most persistent manifestation of sin is to obliterate the memory of sin. This is accomplished by blurring our connection with God. We avoid a detailed awareness of our sin not by claiming perfection or professing blamelessness but by disassociating whatever is wrong with us from a sense of God and renaming it as either ignorance or sickness. The act of renaming is, in fact, obfuscation: it is now no longer apparent that what is wrong with us has anything to do with God. If what is wrong is a matter of our minds (ignorance) or of our bodies (sickness), then we can do something about what is wrong by applying ourselves to education or medicine without ever having to deal with God.

Ignorance is, unarguably, a substantial fact about every human and the cause of much that is wrong with the world and with us. Accurate knowledge is a means for living better. This has been translated into the most extensive system of schooling that the world has ever seen. Sickness also is, unarguably, a substantial fact in every human and the cause of much that is wrong with the world and with us. If we were never sick or disabled we would act more efficiently. This has been translated into an impressive medical establishment. Schools and hospitals have replaced churches (that is, places of prayer) as the dominant locations for taking care of what is wrong with us.

Yet, with all our wonderful schools and our amazing hospitals people don't seem to have gotten any better. They are more learned, they are healthier, but their lives have, if anything, deteriorated. Well-educated and well-doctored, they divorce one another at an alarming rate, use drugs with mind-boggling frequency, and spend their money and time in the pursuit of trivialities that astound the angels.

There is apparently, something wrong with us that the professors and physicians are helpless in doing anything about. That something is sin.

Sin is not what is wrong with our minds; it is the catastrophic disorder in which we find ourselves at odds with God. This is the human condition. The facts of this disorder are all around and within us, but we would prefer to forget them. To remember them is also to remember God, and to remember God is to have to live strenuously, vigorously, and in love. We have moments when we desire to do this, but the moments don't last long. We would rather play golf. We would rather take another battery of tests at the hospital. We would rather take another course at the university. We keep looking for ways to improve our lives without dealing with God. But we can't do it.

When we pray, we immerse ourselves in the living presence of God. When we pray the Psalms we pray through all the parts of our lives and our history and cover the ground of our intricate implication in sin. We acquire a colorful lexicon of words by which we recognize our detailed involvement in the race's catastrophic separation from God: rebel, wanderer, lawless, evil-doer, guilty, liar, fool, corrupt, wicked. The seven "penitential psalms" (6, 32, 38, 51, 102, 130, 143) are the most famous for bringing us to this awareness but hardly a psalm goes by that does not bring another detail of our sin out of the shadows of our practiced forgetfulness.

Like G. K. Chesterton's Father Brown, who was able to solve all crimes because "he had done them all himself," the person at prayer experiences all mercy because he or she has committed all the sins that call down judgement and release forgiveness.

Most of the sins that we do not commit are not because of our virtue, but because we lack either energy or opportunity. We would sin a great deal more than we do if we were only energetic enough and were provided more generous opportunities. It is well to stay in touch with those sins that we would have committed if we had had the chance. The Psalms extend our memory to not only the sins that we have committed but to those we would have if we had not been so tired at the time.

The Country of Salvation

The third area of recovery is a feel for the country of salvation. If creation is the north pole of our memory and sin the south pole, salvation is the seven seas and five continents between. We commonly have no idea of how large it is and how many lifetimes it would take to explore it. It is habitual with us to imagine salvation as something either momentary or occasional—a special intervention in which God makes sure of the eternal disposition of our souls. But it is total. It is comprehensive. It is world embracing, history girdling, life penetrating.

Prayer explores the country of salvation, tramping the contours, smelling the flowers, touching the outcroppings. There is more to do than recognize the sheer fact of salvation and give witness to it: there are unnumbered details of grace, of mercy, of blessing to be appreciated and savored. Prayer is the means by which we do this.

The Psalms take us through the country: they refuse to let us remain parochial in our experience of salvation. They resist the banalizing of salvation into a slogan or password. They bring our good creation and our experienced sin into the action of God, saving action that gathers everything into its operations. Salvation leaves nothing out. Salvation is not a religious compartment, insulated from secularism; it is an energetic, imaginative and relentless invasion of the secular and profane with the announced intention of reclaiming the whole country for love.

Nothing prayed is left outside the action. In prayer we are never left with a reassuring memory of our good creation; we are never left with the disturbing memory of our catastrophic sin; we are always caught up into an action that saves—restores all our relationships into actions of faith and hope and love with God.

The vocabulary of salvation is extensive: save, deliver, ransom, redeem, help, restore, rescue, heal. The verbs are festooned with an endless succession of metaphors: "brought up my soul from Sheol" (30:3), "loosed my sackcloth and girded me with gladness' (30:11), "keeps all his bones" (34:20), "cover him with favor as with a shield" (5:12), "drew me out of many waters" (18:16), "feasted as with marrow and fat" (63:5), "escaped as a bird from the snare of the fowlers" (124:7), "sets the prisoners free" (146.7). Nothing the human can imagine is exempt from this saving action of God. No place is inaccessible to its will:

> If I ascend to heaven, thou art there!
> If I make my bed in Sheol, thou art there! (139:8)

"Forget not all his benefits" is the pivot sentence in the showcase salvation psalm, Psalm 103. The noun *g'mul*, benefit, is embedded in an action: an action of God is bringing or has brought something to a ripe finish. That, in fact, is what all of God's actions do. They work through the confused complexities of this tangled country of creation and sin to bring us and the country to a completed finish, a whole conclusion. The evidence—*g'mulim*, benefits—when we look around sharply and attentively is everywhere. But it is easy to overlook the benefits for very often more immediately before our eyes are projects not yet finished, the works-in-progress that the God of our salvation is engaged in. But if we "forget the benefits," we are only aware of our own efforts, our puny self-help efforts at making the best of a bad deal, our haphazard attempts at capitalizing on the chances available to us. If we "forget the benefits," we slip into what the psychologists label "sensory deprivation" and are deaf, dumb, and blind to the incessant, dynamic, flourishing salvation work that constitutes the dominant action in the country.

Most of our lives consists in what God has done—creating us, speaking to us, loving us. If we are not able to remember any of this, we are bereft of the richest dimensions of our being. A medical indication of brain damage is to be aware only of immediate stimuli and immediate sensations, which is to say, to be without memory. Prayerless, we speak gibberish. Often it is a very learned gibberish, but it is gibberish all the same. Language requires syntax, connections between all the parts of speech. If we are ignorant or forgetful of the many parts, we will speak pig Latin, no matter how many university degrees we hold.

A Mountain of Meaning

Memory is the mysterious capacity we have for gathering the fragments of experience into a large context that is comprehensive and coherent. A life of mere sense impressions has no coherence—it is merely a sequence of stimulus-response occurrences. Prayerless we repeat a dreary round of pious, or not so pious, emotions. Nothing "adds up" in such a life. No meaning accumulates. Prayer develops our memory with God: "connections slowly emerge. Like distant landmarks you are approaching, cause and effect begin to align themselves, draw closer together. Experiences too indefinite of outline in themselves to be recognized connect and are identified as a larger shape. And suddenly a light is thrown back—as when your train makes a curve, showing that there has been a mountain of meaning rising behind you on the way you've come, is rising there still, proven now through retrospect."[6] Memory is the capacity of the human spirit to connect the experience of last year with the one of yesterday, and at the same time to anticipate next week, and next year. The Psalms by training our memories, establish connections with the deepest experiences of which we are capable, which we "have loved long since and lost awhile," as John Henry Newman put it so well.[7]

It becomes evident as we do this that memory is not nostalgia. Memory is not an orientation to the past; it is vigorously present tense, selecting out of the storehouse of the past, retrieving and arranging images and insights, and then hammering them together for use in the present moment. St. Augustine found that the best model for developing the integrating experience of past, present, and future was the audible praying of a psalm.[8] The psalmists exercise their and our memories vigorously. Prayer is an act of memory. If we confine ourselves to one-generational knowledge here, or even worse, to our own conversion-experience knowledge, we are impoverished beyond reason.

Sing praises to the Lord, O you his saints,
   and give thanks to his holy name.
For his anger is but for a moment,
   but his favor is for a lifetime.
Weeping may tarry for the night,
   but joy comes with the morning.

PSALM 30:4–5

Truly I say to you, there are some standing here who will not
taste death before they see the kingdom of God come with
power.

JESUS (MARK 9:1)

What we call the beginning is often the end
And to make an end is to make a beginning.
The end is where we start from.

.   .   .   .

We shall not cease from exploration
And the end of all our exploring
Will be to arrive where we started
And know the place for the first time.

T. S. ELIOT

10. End

The end of prayer is praise. The Psalms show praise as the end of prayer in both meanings of the word: the terminus, the last word in the final Psalm 150; and the goal at which all the psalm-prayers arrive after their long travels through the unmapped back countries of pain, doubt, and trouble, with only occasional vistas of the sunlit lands, along the way.

This last word is also, most significantly, the first word. The verb "praise" *(halel)* in its noun form *(tehillim)* furnishes the title to our prayer book. "Book of Praises" *(sepher tehillim)* is the Hebrew title to the 150 prayers that we commonly name "The Psalms." "Psalms," the title given in our English translations, is from the Greek, *psalmoi,* "songs" used in the Septuagint (a Greek translation of the Hebrew Old Testament begun in the third century B.C.).

This title, "Praises," catches our attention because it is inaccurate. Most psalms are complaints. They are calls of help by helpless and hurting men and women. They are wrung out of desperate conditions. The definitive Psalms' scholar, Hermann Gunkel, said that the prayer of complaint was the backbone of the Psalter.[1] How can it be appropriate, then, to name these prayers "Praises"? Is this false advertising, an attractive smile pasted on the cover of a book that contains a lot of pain, doubt, and trouble? Does the title, in order to involve us in what otherwise might repel, misrepresent the basic nature of prayer as something more pleasant than the data of daily experience warrants, a "spoonful of sugar to make the medicine go down"? A life of prayer forces us to deal with the reality of the world and of our own lives at a depth and with an honesty that is quite unheard of by the prayerless, and much of that reality we would certainly avoid if we could. Do we really want to feel this deeply? Do we want to think this far? The Psalms take us to the painful heart of rejections and alienations and guilts that we could live on the surface of much more happily. If we knew that was where prayer takes us would we have ever signed on? Is the title a pious deceit?

"'Praises'' as a title is not statistically accurate but it is accurate all the same. It is accurate because it accurately describes the end, the finished product. All prayer, pursued far enough, becomes praise. Any prayer, no matter how desperate its origin, no matter how angry and fearful the experiences it traverses, ends up in praise. It does not always get there quickly or easily—the trip can take a lifetime—but the end is always praise. "Praises," in fact, is the only accurate title for our prayer book, for it is the goal that shapes the journey: "The end is where we start from."

The end has far greater shaping over our lives than the beginning. That which we are made for is more significant in our development than the biology of our making. In Aristotle's philosophical analysis of causes, it is not the first cause (the kick that gets us going) but the final cause (the lure that pulls us to the finish) that is uniquely and ultimately decisive.[2] We are not intricately engineered genetic chips that when programmed correctly make the economy prosper; we are unfinished creatures, ravenously purpose-hungry, alive with possibilities. For humans the future is the most creative and the most essential aspect of time. Human life is that "paradoxical reality which consists in deciding what we are going to do, therefore in being what we not yet are, in starting to be the future."[3] The Bible spends only a few pages establishing the conditions of our beginnings; and then several hundred pages cultivating in us a taste for the future—immersing us in a narrative in which the future is always impinging on the present, so that we live out of our beginnings and by the means that are in accordance with the reality of our ends. Not only as a child and adolescent but also as an adult, "what I want to be when I grow up" has far more influence on what I say and do and become than the genetic code I received at my conception.

Prayer is our most intense and interior act of futurity. All prayers, by definition, are directed to God, and this aim brings them, finally into the presence of God where "everything that has breath" praises the Lord. Praise is the deep, even if often hidden, eschatological dimension in prayer.[4]

Praise Eruptions

There are intimations of this throughout the Psalms. Not infrequently, in the middle of a terrible lament, defying logic and without transition, praise erupts.

Psalm 13, for instance. Five hard questions are put to God, followed by three petitions underscored by a triple desperation. The prayer is pure lament. There is no evidence in the prayer that even one of the questions is answered; there is no sign that even a first installment is made on granting the petitions; there is no hint that the desperate conditions change into anything less desperate. But abruptly and unaccountably the laments metamorphose into praise:

> But I have trusted in thy steadfast love;
> my heart shall rejoice in thy salvation.
> I will sing to the Lord,
> because he has dealt bountifully with me.

The first and last verbs ("trusted" and "dealt bountifully") are rendered as completed actions, but no experience is set forth to validate them: the experience of the prayer is doubt (expressed in those five questions) and deprivation (expressed in those three petitions). All the same, the two actions are said to have occurred: God "dealt bountifully" and the person "trusted." Where? How? Why? We don't know. Nothing "happened." Yet somehow, in a way never explained but often verified, in the act of praying the worst of things, praise springs forth, fully formed and resplendently armed, like Athena from the head of Zeus: "my heart shall rejoice"; "I will sing." The prayer, for a moment, is in touch with its final end, its completion in praise. "Most joy is anticipatory," says Karl Barth. "It normally has something of an eschatological character."[5]

This kind of thing happens all the time as people pray. Praise, when we least expect, in places we never would have guessed, erupts.[6] There is nothing in psychology or grammar to account of this."Sometimes a light surprises the Christian while he sings; it is the Lord who rises with healing in his wings," as William Cowper puts it. Not surprisingly, this happens a lot in the Psalms. St. Teresa of Avila, who lived a hard life with much sickness, badgered by detractors and misunderstood by friends, confirms the cheerful witness, "The pay begins in this life."[7]

Praising through the Alphabet

This *telos* of praise, embedded in the very nature of prayer, begins to be formalized at Psalm 145. Psalm 145 is given the title Praise *(t'hillah)*, the only prayer in the Psalter so designated. This is the first element in an elaborate and artful finale that brings the Psalms to a conclusion.

Psalm 145 is an anthology, arranged in the form of an acrostic. The twenty-two letters of the Hebrew alphabet form, in turn, the initial letters of quotations and near quotations, imitations and echoes from the previous 144 psalms.[8] The striking feature of this acrostic anthology is not its form (acrostics are not new in the Psalter) but its vigorously singleminded selectivity: each of the entries is a sentence of praise. No lament or complaint is permitted. No confession or perplexity is admitted. It is all praise.

This is remarkable because an acrostic suggests, if not exactly promises, inclusive completeness—everything from A to Z. The Psalms have explored the totality of the human condition before God—the Sheol-depths and the Sirion-heights, the quiet green pastures and the harsh jackel-haunted wastes. In an anthology set as a conclusion we would expect a compendium—a selection of lines that hold before us the enormous range of prayer, the incredibly diverse country that has been climbed and tunneled and trekked. Isn't it important, in conclusion, that we do not lose access to any of this experience, not lose touch with a single syllable in this encyclopedic articulation of our humanity in all its complexity? Instead we get praise, all praise. Like Wallace Stevens's poem in which a blackbird is looked at over and over again, from angle after angle eighteen times, Psalm 145 takes a single subject and says it, with variations, until the alphabet runs out.

The foundations for the conclusion have now been laid: we realize the end of prayer implicit in every beginning prayer, that eucharist is subterranean and will eventually break out no matter what the surface terrain and weather show at the present.

The Final Exuberance

This meticulous acrostic, though, hardly prepares us for what follows: five hallelujah psalms, each more exuberant than the last. This final exuberance is not arbitrarily imposed on the collected psalms to give a suitable and pleasing finish; it is organic to prayer and issues out of its very nature.

Earlier hallelujah psalms (111, 112, 113) were taken up into the celebration of Passover, the great salvation feast that gave focus to all of Israel's prayers in celebrative worship. For Christians this feast takes shape in the Sacrament of the Lord's Supper, called eucharist (Greek for "thanksgiving") after its characteristic prayer of thanksgiving, combining praise and blessing.

Eucharist, then, is the Christian term that gathers up the hallelujahs of Israel that issue out of creation and salvation and follows them to their end, their *telos*, in Christ. Eucharist describes the end, the goal and conclusion of prayer. The eucharistic impulse is internal to prayer, and eventually shows itself.[9]

Prefigurings of this end occur spontaneously as we have noted throughout the psalms (these outbreaks always occur when people pray), but they have also been inserted formally at intervals so that a cumulative expectation of final praise is built into the very structure of the Psalter. At the end of each of the editorially arranged five "books" (1–41, 42–72, 73–89, 90–106, 107–150), there is a praising benediction.

> Blessed be the Lord, the God of Israel,
> from everlasting to everlasting!
> Amen and Amen. (41:13)

> Blessed be his glorious name for ever;
> may his glory fill the whole earth!
> Amen and Amen! (72:19)

> Blessed be the Lord forever!
> Amen and Amen! (89:52)

> Blessed be the Lord, the God of Israel,
> from everlasting to everlasting!
> And let all the people say, "Amen!"
> Praise the Lord! (106:48)

> Let everything that breathes praise the Lord!
> Praise the Lord! (150:6)

The first four benedictions work variations on a common theme with the words "Blessing" and "Amen" holding key positions. Blessing is the initial word establishing, in first place, the promise and expectation of the rich goodness of God spilling over into creation and creatures. A double Amen, nailing down the affirmation of God, his most certain Yes, is the last word. Three times this double Amen is used in identical repetitions (41:13; 72:19; 89:52); the fourth time (106:48) the ante is raised to "Let all the people say, 'Amen!' " The "sense of an ending" is gathering momentum. Then, almost as an afterthought it seems, a Hallelujah ("praise the Lord!") is added. When the time comes to provide a conclusion for the fifth book, the Blessing and the Amen, wonderful and powerful as they are, are dropped in order to bring the Hallelujah front and center as the controlling word. Psalm 150 begins and ends with Hallelujah, but also uses it internally. These hallelujahs are cannonades: thirteen times this strongest of all Hebrew praise words thunders across the earth reverberating the eucharistic end of prayer.

There is more. Psalm 150 does not stand alone; four more hallelujah psalms are inserted in front of it so that it becomes the fifth of five psalms that conclude the Psalter—five hallelujah psalms, one for each "book" of the Psalms, and the last, the 150th doing double duty as the conclusion to both the fifth book and to the five books all together.

These five hallelujah psalms are extraordinarily robust. They put all the acts of God's salvation and deliverance, his creation and providence on display and festoon them with hallelujah garlands. They put the sounds of the hallelujah into wind and water, widow and orphan, ravens and angels, lute and harp, sea monsters and saints. The five hallelujah psalms with Psalm 145 as a foundation are a cathedral built entirely of praise. No matter how much we suffer, no matter our doubts, no matter how angry we get, no matter how many times we have asked in desperation or doubt, "How long?", prayer develops finally into praise. Everything finds its way to the doorstep of praise. Praise is the consummating prayer. This is not to say that other prayers are inferior to praise, only that all prayer pursued far enough, becomes praise.

This architectonic form, besides assuring completeness also suggests that there are no shortcuts. The thoughtful and painstaking process of selecting, arranging, and concluding is the exact antithesis of glibness. This is not a "word of praise" slapped onto whatever mess we are in at the moment. This crafted conclusion for the Psalms tells us that our prayers are going to end in praise, but that it is also going to take awhile. Don't rush it. It may take years, decades even, before certain prayers arrive at the hallelujahs, at Psalms 146–150 with their acrostic foundation in Psalm 145. Not every prayer is capped off with praise. In fact most prayers, if the Psalter is a true guide, are not. But prayer, a praying life, finally becomes praise. Prayer is always reaching towards praise and will finally arrive there. If we persist in prayer, laugh and cry, doubt and believe, struggle and dance and then struggle again, we will surely end up at Psalm 150, on our feet, applauding, "Encore! Encore!"[10]

Like the notes of music that anticipate melodic completion by
notes yet to come, prayer has this element of futurity always in
it, pulling us to the region of completion, the region of glory
and praise.[11] The future is not a blank to be filled in, depending
on our mood, by either fantasy or horror, but a source of brightness that we await and receive. Our lives are still outstanding.
Our prayers give expression to lives that go far beyond the past
and present and reach into what is promised and prophesied.
When we pray we can no longer confine our understanding of
ourselves to who we are or have been; we understand ourselves
in terms of possibilities yet to be realized—in St. Paul's phrase,
"the glory yet to be revealed."

And so the Psalms come to an end, a resounding conclusion
with all the prayer experiences of men and women who risk
their lives in the venture of faith, gathered into praise. The end
of prayer, all prayer, any prayer, is praise. Our lives fill out in
goodness; earth and heaven meet in an extraordinary conjunc-
tion. Clashing cymbals announce the glory: Blessing. Amen.
Hallelujah.

Appendix: Reports from the Field

From time to time, as I have opportunity and it seems appropriate, I ask people who have embarked on a monthly cycle of praying the Psalms to write down what they are experiencing in following this ancient and common practice of praying Christians. In my guidance I suggest that after praying the Psalms for ten or fifteen minutes, another five or ten minutes be spent with a journal, writing whatever is there in the mind and spirit (not trying to comment on the psalm or explain it), using the journal to pay attention to oneself, the praying person answering God.

I include here a sampler from what I have received. I offer it as evidence—"reports from the field"—of what happens as the Psalms are embraced as our basic prayer text. Some are from people in my congregation, others from students in courses I have taught in universities and seminaries, others from persons I have never met who have responded to something I have written; these are conversational and personal "field notes" collected from friends as we pursue a life of prayer in companionship with the Psalms.

Thank you, Eugene, for helping me to learn to pray the Psalms this summer. God really got me out of the cocoon of church staff life, where I was bolstered daily on every side by like-minded Christians, and into the world of business—that world of self which you recommend "unselfing." What a positively stretching experience it is to move as a Christian through that world, but not allowing it into the center. I am learning to pray about *everything* and most especially about clients and situations which are difficult sometimes to the point of being repulsive. But I know that God can and is using me more effectively in this setting than he ever could while I was ensconced in my cozy little church office.

I'm listening. I've been praying the Psalms. But I've been experiencing the same distance from them as from Jesus. I have come face-to-face with how difficult it is for me to extract meaning from prayer. Perhaps the word "extract" is a tip-off. The course itself and the psalms praying suggest that there's nothing to wrest from the cosmos, that it's all there, that it has been from the beginning of time. I feel like a nut in search of cracking, only to suspect my shell is like the emperor's new clothes.

I want Christ. Although it's a bit scary for me to say that. I don't fear God; I don't know what it means. Trembling awe is quite comprehensible to me, but not mine—yet? I'm in conflict. I want to meditate, emptying myself in noble apophatic fashion. The Psalms are not finished with me? [My] deep-rooted suspicion . . . is that I'm an outsider in faith or that my homemade brand will not carry me home. So long as this is the case, much of the Christian theology will ring hollow to me. Without the central act of faith in Christ I am doing much wheel spinning. I want to contemplate Jesus, but I feel I must meet him first.

There seems little more to say—I have come to the water's edge of faith. In the pool is my God and my Life, the Word. It matters not whether I do a swan dive or steal over the edge. But I act as one who has never seen the water, yearning for it and not sure what to do. I will sit at the edge. I will read from the Psalms. And at a time when all is right I will find myself alive and wet. That much faith I have.

My own experience and belief is that all areas—mind, feelings, behavior, spirit—are essential parts of us as humans. A major part of my task as a therapist is to encourage the ownership and celebration of the totality of persons. The people I see, all too often, claim only what they see as the negative parts of themselves.

The Psalms became part of my prayer life in the mid 70's during a time I was struggling for physical health and with a severe clinical depression. It was during this time that I first discovered Dietrich Bonhoeffer's work, and I took note of his stated practice of including a New Testament reading and a reading from the Psalms in his daily prayer practice. I began to do the same and found in the Psalms more empathy for the darkness I was experiencing than anywhere else I'd turned. A divorce after twenty-six years of marriage cast me adrift in a new way—adrift from social and church moorings of many years.

The Psalms became an incredible treasure in the healing/ growing, identifying, and ownership process I was experiencing. I came to be able to look behind my exterior mask of "all's right with the world" and to learn to pray from the pit.

I have not always been quiet in my praying of the Psalms, often furious at God for the loneliness and brokenness. Yet it is impossible to be angry and frustrated with a God you do not believe is there or have a dynamic relationship with. He knows my feelings, and the Psalms continue to affirm my acknowledgment of them to him. They affirm the depth and height of the emotional, physical, and spiritual experiences I have become free enough to own and experience, and have made clear to me that God intends that, as humans, we are called to explore our humanness to its fullest. Psalmic Theatre.

For quite a spell I have been seeking something which will assist me and bring me onto a journey of becoming, of being the essential human self God has destined me for. Being presented with the Psalter has disclosed the roots of this growth, the base from which I can by grace learn to live deliberately and holistically to God's glory. By means of the course, the readings, and the initial practice of "Praying the Psalms," I am realizing the elemental necessity not only for an inclusive centering spiritual life which radiates and enters the world, transforming it, but also that of daily psalm praying as the prime tool for my training—asceticism.

My actual praying of the Psalms has gone well, though with a few disappointments, usually with myself for missing a day or an inclination to doubt and lose confidence in the practice. Here the meditation on the tree metaphor or Psalm 1 is encouraging. I found that a background of study, such as from class, is especially helpful as it "takes off the blanket" making the Psalms become alive, meaningful, and relational in my prayer. A balance of these two modes is essential for the authentication of each: prayer to become; study to illuminate the "story." I soon discovered the necessity to disengage myself from emotional climates and moods, not to be at their mercy, but not to ignore them either. Part of our sacrifices are such emotions, good or bad, laying them on the altar for God to direct or redirect. The rhythms of the Psalms take time to discover the poetic breath. I also have found the rhythm of the Hebraic day useful. I step into the best far more easily when I adopt the evening (Psalm 4) and morning (Psalm 5) psalms to my rule. My hope is that by God's grace I will be given fortitude and tenacity . . . To continue, to envelop the Psalter as my own in and out of the communion of saints; to read/say them out of obedience rather than for egocentric returns.

One aspect of the class that was especially beneficial was learning to keep a journal. Crystallizing my thoughts and reading through the Psalms helped me to recognize some thought patterns and rhythms in my life that had not been evident before. It was especially insightful to submit to the rhythm and the words, to read out loud. And then to write three or four minutes of reflections on the Psalms gave me an understanding [of] the ebb and the tide that I felt was present. The assignment also afforded me the benefit of formulating thoughts about scripture into words I had not exercised previously. I recognized that praying through the entire book of Psalms in one month was too fast for me, and that I was thankful that my notes would not be read by anyone else. I didn't even really like reading them myself but the exercise of writing down the reflections was illuminating to me. The words were not so significant . . . But the absorption of the Psalms was creating in me a relationship with David and the Holy Spirit that I had not felt before. The hardest lesson that I . . . learned was to be critical, not only to my husband and my son and myself but to God and to others. It is not my nature to be critical. Thus finding fault, allowing anger to surface, admitting hate were not new concepts to me, but they were original in that I had not allowed them to be manifest in my personality. Being able to tell God that I hate someone is actually quite revolutionary to me. I had always believed that if I felt anything negative toward anyone that it was wrong [that I should] not admit those feelings. But this class gave me a new perspective on dealing with the feelings that the Lord has given us. I don't believe that I have worked through this concept thoroughly, but it is definitely a new stepping stone in my journey of faith.

One of the key things that praying the Psalms has sensitized me to is how much our individualistic and technological society works against any inclinations we may have to engage in intimate, gut-level dialogue with God.

Having spent more than half of my life in school being fed information, and four years in college learning specifically how to use motivational language to manipulate people into buying things (I was a media/marketing major), learning that the Psalms have been used throughout the church's history as tools to train the church in the conversion of language hit me with revolutionary force. It makes sense, in our print-oriented society, that the word of God should come to be seen as a static collection of recorded words, rather than a dynamic oral dialogue in which God continues to speak and we continue to answer.

It has been exciting to discover that using the Psalms to pray connects us with the struggles and responses of all of God's people throughout history. And how, in our fast-paced and noisy society, praying the Psalms can slow us down and cause us to tune into the softer rhythms of nature which are often snuffed out in our frenzy of activity.

In my experience of praying the Psalms, I have felt as if I have suddenly been given the ears to hear the dialogue that has been going on between God and man and to find myself as a participant in the conversation. I have found that praying the Psalms has taken the focus of my prayer off of my needs and ability to do, and put it unto *God's* power and activity. I have come to see the Psalms as a guide to reciting the particularities of the battle God is waging against the enemies of his people.

As I speak the words of the psalmist, my story merges with his story, widening my perception of God and self beyond my own subjective feelings. In the Psalms, I can see the transformation of the psalmist's anger and hostility as God gives him new hope and strength. Although at the moment I am praying I may not be experiencing the intensity of pain the psalmist is, reciting his words lessens my fear about the prospects of being in a situation of suffering because I am encouraged by how God has worked in the psalmist's life. Likewise, when I find myself praying a psalm of joy on a day when I feel sad, I am able to hold onto the hope of the psalmist and remember the times God has done great things in my life.

Although praying the Psalms every day over the past few weeks has given me a real sense of the discipline which flows from seeing the Psalms as a way of connecting myself with God's historical community, I have not yet begun to speak the language myself with deep emotion or let its rhythms flow through my whole person. I must still mature in the area of letting the Psalms become a means of praying out my anger and hostility and slowing me down in the midst of the craziness of life.

In the past few weeks, God has expanded my understanding of prayer and spirituality. He has cleared up some misconceptions and given me insight through lectures and readings. More importantly, though, he has met me in prayer and in a new way through the Psalms. My experience of God's presence has broadened, and my desire to mature spiritually has deepened as I have prayed the Psalms.

I have been able to embrace the earthly in my own life much more deeply than before. I have begun to pay attention to my own "animal" nature, appreciating the rhythms of activity and rest, work and play. I have begun to see God's grace more clearly in nature and have allowed myself to receive that grace. I enjoy the variety of sights, smells, tastes, and feelings available to me each day. This simple openness to my earthly nature has enriched my relationship to God, allowing me to relate to him throughout the day, not only during "prayer time."

Because our *relationship* to God is so fundamental to our Christian faith, it is important that we protect and nurture it. The Psalms provide a language in which to do this. Through them I learn to express not only ideas and information (which God knows anyway), I learn to express emotions and to nurture relationship. It is not necessary that I tell God in prayer everything that I do each day, or that I bring every possible prayer concern before him. Rather, I must tell him how I feel and respond to the events of the day and bring before him prayers that are truly my concern. The Psalms teach me to do this. No psalm is comprehensive, expressing all truth and all emotional possibilities; instead, each psalm explores a particular truth and expresses fully a particular emotion. Only taken together do they express the broadest range of truth and emotion.

Praying the Psalms has expanded my view of spirituality and of prayer itself. I have begun to see my spirituality as a broadly defined way of being, rather than as a limited aspect of my life. I have begun to express emotion freely, while relying on God's constancy and eternal character to provide my primary focus. Finally, I have actually begun to experience and practice a way of being based on a close and intimate relationship with God.

While I was trying to pray the Psalms out loud, I found it difficult to concentrate in them. I felt I did not even find rhythm or musicality in them as they were supposed to have. I then hardly found joy in them as I used to a few years ago. My mind had become very analytical and my heart somewhat insensitive along the last months. This might be due, in part, to the tremendous change of my life: about a year ago I was teaching in Colombia and did not know that I would be intensely studying in a graduate school and living in another very different culture. I have been exposed to a great amount of intellectual information and reflection but I feel I have not "digested" it slowly. I feel overwhelmed and tired. Everything has been very fast.

When reading the Psalms then, I was bringing this mind to them and what I think I might have been reading in them was my own drought. As I was reflecting on this matter, I became aware of the influence of this consumerist and "wastepaper" society on my way of approaching scripture. My study of the Psalms is subjected to "my" needs (how effectively the Word works), "my" time (time is no more God's but "mine".—one of the most "popular" expressions of individualism) and "my" mind (what my intellect may understand and interpret out of it). I realized . . . I was held in a tension between a "functional" mind and a lonely soul. The word contemplation did not seem to have any meaning in this context. It does not sound practical at all. I noticed I had forgotten my former times of communion with God when my lifestyle was more simple. I also found that I was reproducing the same attitude of "consuming" academic information when studying scripture. It was hard to delight in simply reading the Psalms out loud then.

However, since I tried to keep reading and "meditating" about the Psalms every day, I found out that the psalmist has the freedom to express his spiritual emptiness and frustration to God. I found how the first step for intimacy is honesty. It also struck me that this intimacy is wrapped up in the use of a "primary" language in which the imperatives, the cry for help and the open expression of emotions like anger, sadness, hatred, desperation, etc., are not only allowed but exposed without any reluctancy. This . . . led me to think about my own barriers in prayer. For example, since my emotions of anger were suppressed at a very early age, because they were considered as bad, I have a hard time in expressing anger to God and I generally become depressed and sad. Similarly, this happens with primary attitudes like commands, dislikes, etc.

I observe the psalmist as a very healthy person in an intimate and free relationship with God. I realize how much I need to grow in this matter. I want to learn how to pray my hatred and enjoy this freedom of recognizing, accepting, and communicating my feelings with transparency. I also suspect that since the Psalms were prayed in community, the expression of primary language is not then . . . a private attempt but a communal experience of God's people.

It is fascinating to find that I can break my own emotional restrictions when praying: I do not have to say nice things all the time if this is not what I really feel. I can take risks in being honest with God [and] my father and avoid projecting my own feelings for my father to God. Now I can distinguish better the similarities and differences between my two fathers.

I am a "keeper" by nature. ınnkeepers, bookkeepers, housekeepers, keepers in general, all devote long hours, if not their very lives, to the protection and maintenance, the care and nurture of what is "kept." So it seemed a natural step that I became keeper of my spiritual estate the moment I murdered my childhood God.

Early on I had confused relationship to the infinite God with my finite ideas about God. In the crisis of being that followed, God died with my ideas. Abandoned, I grew increasingly angry and defiant. Prayer became an act of shaking my fist in the face of God and damning him for giving me a mind—a weapon capable of deicide, a weapon by which he consented to die and orphan me.

Unwilling to accept the death of my childhood God, I set his corpse in my living room and prayed at it thinking I might resurrect it by merely screaming, "Speak to me!" I eventually grew weary of futile effort. Gathering the tattered remains of my puppet God, I tossed them in a back room, locked the door, and became a keeper of spiritual garbage.

I then retreated into isolation, content to lick my wounds while taking refuge once again in intellectual constructs and the vast world of religious ideas. But mental gymnastics was a poor substitute for relationship with the living God and the pain of separation had left me hollow and cynical. How desperately I longed for the elusive "hearing" that would cleanse and heal the vacuous ache at the core of me.

After four years of constant battling and retreating, I gave up. I surrendered my role as keeper gave a proper burial to my childhood God, and timidly opened my front door to the unknown.

In the convalescent months that followed I gradually became aware of a tender mystery weaving itself around and through me. For the first time in so many pain-filled years I slowly began to hear God. "Listen," said a voice without words. "Just wait, be still, and listen." I rooted myself in fertile silence and waited. "I love you," said the voice without words. I was shattered. The pain I had felt—feeling abandoned, unheard, cut off—was turned on me as I met God's pain at my absence and touched the edge of the depth of his longing for communion with me. Gentle arms of grace tenderly gathered the battered and wounded fragments of me into a healing embrace of permeating love. No longer responsible for my own keeping, I was free to be "kept" by God.

I had been extravagantly, powerfully restored to right relationship. I thankfully celebrated the reconciliation but I knew enough not to be seduced by its sweetness. Soon the party would end and the work of healing and restoration would begin. But how to begin? During my years in spiritual exile I had deteriorated into a functional illiterate in the language of prayer. I was willing to start back at square one, but what was it?

In these twelve post reconciliation months, a stab-in-the-dark, hit-and-miss approach has characterized my prayer. Mostly I pray small prayers about not knowing how to pray and ask for guidance. I know how to cry for help in the midst of crisis, but in the day-to-day work of relationship I flounder through a routine of sophomoric babbling.

Disenchanted with going it alone and hungry for guidance, I enrolled in your class determined to submit my context to the content of the course and abandon, embrace, change, whatever would be required.

The fact that prayer is primarily a responsive act gave a whole new perspective to my years of screaming at God. Unwilling to acknowledge what God had already spoken, I demanded that he speak to me from the script I had written. If I couldn't write the God lines in my own story, I wasn't going to participate. Nothing else was acceptable. The ensuing silence then was not a cessation of speech on God's part but an unwillingness on my part to hear anything I couldn't control. The mere shifting in my understanding of prayer as a response to what God had already spoken made years of painful ambiguity and struggle suddenly clear and meaningful.

When praying the Psalms I think that perspective is a by-product of memory. When I first prayed the Psalms and recorded my thoughts as you instructed, my first sentence was, "I read and memories come." Continuing, I wrote, "The context I bring to my reading—the painful memories, the anxiety, fear, loneliness—are all intensified when I bring them to the Psalms. The Psalms take me excruciatingly deeper into the core of me in my present context—there is no room for abstraction or escape."

In class when the statement "Alone with God is not good" came thundering across my Isolation River, it knocked me off my feet. I landed with a thud on the muddy riverbank and I knew this would be a tough one for me to cross. In fact, I have yet to stand up and get my feet wet. And what's worse, I know that this is one of those rivers I'll need to cross again and again.

Abandoning isolation and embracing community is particularly difficult because it violates my independent "keeper" nature. It was hard enough to relinquish my keeper role to the infinite God—the thought of consistently entrusting myself to a community of other flawed believers strikes me as mildly horrifying. Plus, I feel like I haven't a clue about what that practically means.

But the Psalms, and you, seem to say that, if nothing else, a clue is what I do have.

In praying the Psalms I am rescued from the tyranny of ruts and routines and nurtured instead in the arms of ritual and rhythm. The Psalms are the tools that transform the rut of my hit-and-miss prayer into daily portions of sustaining grace; they rescue me from drowning in the fatal mechanics of routine and safely usher me into the life-giving waters of rhythm. Equipped with these requisite tools, there is nothing left but to dig into the details—the gnawing, nasty, realities of growth and relationship.

Conclusion? I don't suppose there really is one. But I do now know that in the practice of submitting my prayer to the Psalms I am sustained by the keeper of my soul, the initiating God who all my life long has been guiding, protecting, nurturing, and loving me into being.

Notes

Introduction

1. In the fourth century in Bethlehem, Jerome's close friend, Paula, wrote a letter to Marcella, asking her to flee from Rome to the solitude of Christ's village. In her description of the life of prayer that she and her daughter Eustochium lived there with a few companions she called the Psalms "our implements of husbandry", which is close to my metaphor, "tools." (Quoted by Rowland E. Prothero in *The Psalms in Human Life* [London: John Murray, 1903], 12.)

2. The eminent Psalms scholar, A. F. Kirkpatrick, demonstrated their "paramount importance in the history of Christian worship and devotion" in his commentary. He made the bold claim that "if a history of the use of the Psalter could be written, it would be a history of the spiritual life of the Church. From the earliest times the Psalter has been the Church's manual of Prayer and Praise in its public worship, the treasury of devotion for its individual members in their private communing with God." (A. F. Kirkpatrick, *The Book of Psalms*, 1st edition [Cambridge, England: Cambridge University Press, 1957], xcviii.)

   Louis Bouyer provides witness from another angle: "The Psalter [is] our fundamental prayer. For the Psalter is also, in its way, a prayer of man which is at the same time the Word of God. If we wish, therefore, to give to God's word the most faithful and most obedient answer in our prayer, we must use above any other that prayer which continues in the mouth of man to be the Word of God." (Louis Bouyer, *Life and Liturgy* [London: Sheed and Ward, 1962], 230.)

   Dietrich Bonhoeffer, during the years in which he gave leadership to the clandestine theological community at Finkenwalde, standing against the "take-over" of the churches by Hitler, set the Psalms at the center: "*From ancient times in the Church a special significance has been attached to the common use of psalms.* In many churches to this day the Psalter constitutes the beginning of every service of common worship. The custom has been largely lost and *we must find our way back to its prayers.*" Emphasis mine. (Dietrich Bonhoeffer, *Life Together* [New York: Harper and Brothers, 1954], 44.)

   Baron Friedrich von Hügel, among the wisest of twentieth century spiritual masters, corroborates the witness. In a letter to his niece, Gwendolyne Greene, whom he was guiding in a life of prayer, he wrote: "In this as in so much else I find that you are one with the church, that you pray the psalms" (*Letters from Baron Friedrich von Hügel to a Niece*, Gwendolen Greene, ed. [London: J. M. Dent and Sons, 1958], 185.)

3. Martin Luther is representative: "The Psalter is the book of all saints; and

everyone, in whatever situation he may be, finds in that situation psalms and words that fit his case, that suit him as if they were put there just for his sake, so that he could not put it better himself, or find or wish for anything better." (*Word and Sacrament I*, vol. 35 of *Luther's Works* [Philadelphia: Fortress Press, 1960], 255–56.)

4. Denise Levertov, *The Poet in the World* (New York: New Directions Publishing Corp., 1973), 243.

5. Augustine *Enarratio in Psalm 85*, J. P. Migne, ed., *Patrologia Latina* (Paris, 1845).

6. Commentaries, though, are splendid companions. The best general introduction that I know of for the praying Christian is Walter Brueggemann, *The Message of the Psalms* (Minneapolis: Augsburg Publishing House, 1984).

7. John Calvin, *Commentary on the Book of Psalms* (Grand Rapids, MI: William B. Eerdmans Publishing Co., 1949, 1. 334).

8. Benedict's exact words: "That the mind may echo in harmony with the voice." ("The Rule of St. Benedict," in *Western Asceticism*, ed. Owen Chadwick [Philadelphia: Westminister Press, 1958], 309.

Chapter 1: Text

Epigraph: Michael Fishbane, *Text and Texture* (New York: Schocken Books, 1979), 141.

1. "What difference does it make to the content of the psalms that they are poems? . . . Poetry, working through a system of complex linkages of sound, image, word, rhythm, syntax, theme, idea, is an instrument for conveying densely patterned meanings, and sometimes contradictory meanings, that are not readily conveyable through other kinds of discourse. . . . poetry is the most complex ordering of language, and perhaps also the most demanding. Within the formal limits of a poem the poet can take advantage of the emphatic repetitions dictated by the particular prosodic systems, the symmetries and antithesis and internal intertwinings of sound and image and reported act, the modulated shifts in grammatical voice and object of address, to give coherence and authority to his perceptions of the world. The psalmist's delight in the suppleness and serendipities of poetic form is not a distraction from spiritual seriousness of the poems but his chief means of realizing his spiritual vision, and it is one source of the power these poems continue to have not only to excite our imaginations but also to engage our lives." (Robert Alter, *The Art of Biblical Poetry* [New York: Basic Books, Inc., 1985], 113, 136.)

2. Calvin, Commentary, 1. xxxvii.

3. A young woman was pouring out before me the mess of her life. She was not a member of my congregation and did not profess the Christian faith, but there was some quality in her narration that caught my attention. I interrupted, "Kerry, do you ever pray?" Her response was quick: "No. Never." I waited. There was just the flicker of a smile; she qualified her denial: "Sometimes I wish upwards." It was, I thought, a remarkably discerning distinction.

4. "If the doors of perception were cleansed every thing would appear to man as it is, infinite." (William Blake, *Selected Poetry and Prose* [New York: The Modern Library, 1953], 129.)

Chapter 2: Way

Epigram: T. S. Eliot, "East Coker," in *The Complete Poems and Plays 1901–1950* (New York: Harcourt, Brace and Co., 1958), 127.

1. "What enables man to know anything at all about the world around him? 'Knowing demands the organ fitted to the object,' said Plotinus (died A.D. 270). Nothing can be known without there being an appropriate 'instrument' in the makeup of the knower. This is the Great Truth of 'adaequatio' (adequateness), which defines knowledge as *adaequatio rei et intellectus*—the understanding of the knower must be adequate to the thing to be known." (E. F. Schumacher, *A Guide for the Perplexed* [New York: Harper & Row, 1977], 39.)

2. St. John of the Cross is relentless in insisting on this basic truth in the life of prayer and frequently cites Thomas Aquinas ("the philosopher") as his authority: "As the philosopher says, whatever is received is received according to the mode of the receiver." He then elaborates: "Since these natural faculties do not have the purity, strength, or capacity to receive and taste supernatural things in a supernatural or divine mode, but only according to their own mode which is human and lowly, as we said, these faculties must also be darkened regarding the divine so that weaned, purged, and annihilated in their natural way they might lose that lowly and human mode of receiving and working. Thus all these faculties and appetites of the soul are tempered and prepared for the sublime reception, experience, and savor of the divine and supernatural, which is unreceivable until the old man dies." (*The Collected Works of St. John of the Cross*, trans. Kieran Kavanaugh, O.C.D. and Otilio Rodriquez, O.C.D., [Washington, D.C., Institute of Caramelite Studies, 1979], 364.)

This is an almost entirely ignored truth in our day. We therefore require remedial tutoring in the epistemology of prayer. The citation of a few witnesses will serve to emphasize how fundamental and necessary this is, and at the same time show that Psalms 1 and 2 need to be taken far more seriously than they commonly are as exercises that equip us to pray:

William Blake: "A fool sees not the same tree that a wise man sees." (*Selected Poetry and Prose* [New York: The Modern Library, 1953], 125.)

Edwin Chargaff: "We take from others only what we already have in ourselves." (*Heraclitian Fire*, [New York: The Rockefeller University Press, 1978], 111.)

Thorlief Boman: "It is worth noting how Plato exerts himself to make clear that the intuition of the higher and particularly of the highest form of beauty depends upon whether the man is willing to pay the price of toil, sacrifice, and renunciation which is required; the Israelite must pay a similar price to get God's blessing (Psalms 15, 24:3ff). The soul of the beholder must therefore gradually be changed so that it is likened to the constantly ascending forms of beauty." (*Hebrew Thought Compared with Greek* [New York: W. W. Norton & Co., 1970], 86.

Anaïs Nin: "We don't see things as they are, we see them as we are."

Lacordaire: "Everyone looks at what I look at, but no one sees what I see." (Quoted by Pierre Lacoque, *The Jonah Complex* [Atlanta: John Knox Press, 1981], 104.

Jesus: "Blessed are the pure in heart, for they shall see God." (Matthew 5:8)

W. R. Inge: "We can only know a thing by becoming it." (*Christian Mysticism* [New York: Meridian Books, 1956], 93.)

Amos Wilder: "The insights and metamorphoses of the self associated with ecstasy are related to prior disciplines. I would suppose that neither Einstein's clarifying formula nor Dante's vision of the rose in the Paradiso were presented to them on a silver platter while they idled. No doubt meditation and a wise passivity and negative capability were involved, but also years of intense application. If this law holds for the genius it also holds for the rest of us. We cannot shortcut divine wisdom by manipulation, nor should we confuse psychic pyrotechnics with the fulfillments of a long period of gestation. . . . Under the influence of black coffee and brandy at midnight sophomores have become Platos and Shakespeares and have been granted the ultimate secrets of the universe—but in the morning their scribblings were no such matter. Artists and mystics have first to practice their scales and learn their abc's and train their reactions. Inebriation is no substitute for paideia." (*Theopoetics* [Philadelphia: Fortress Press, 1976], 63, 67.)

3. "The noun *torah* is built from the Hiphil, transitive, form of the verb *yarah*. *Yarah* means 'to shoot,' but the Hiphil, while also meaning such, means as well 'to teach.' When one man teaches another, he shoots ideas from his own into the other's mind. But in so doing he 'reveals' what is in his own." (George A. F. Knight, *A Christian Theology of the Old Testament* [Atlanta: John Knox Press, 1959], 237–38. As the word was used it accumulated meanings, and through the centuries of its use it became comprehensive, summing up the entire revelation of God's election and appropriation of Israel. But always there was a liveliness in the word, an action embedded in the noun, that resisted relegation to a bookshelf or a library. See Gerhard von Rad, *Old Testament Theology* (New York: Harper and Brothers, 1962), 1. 221–223. There did take place a "fateful change" (von Rad's phrase) that treated God's revelation as legislation, "law," imposed from the outside rather than instruction that seeks after mature inward assent, but it is nowhere in evidence in the life of prayer. The *Sitz im Leben* of the Torah was, in the Psalms, "more and more the heart of man" (p. 199–200).

4. James Luther Mays, "The Place of the Torah Psalms in the Psalter," *Journal of Biblical Literature* 106 (March 1987): 3.

5. James Luther Mays describes *hagah* as "the kind of study that proceeds orally; it rehearses and repeats. It searches the instruction of God by reciting in receptivity until the matter becomes part of the thinking and willing and doing." (Ibid., 9.)

6. "Transplanted alongside irrigation channels" sounds cobbled in comparison with "planted by streams of water" but the plain sense of the words *shatul palgey mayim* hardly allows for anything else. See C. A. Briggs, *A Critical and Exegetical Commentary on The Book of Psalms* (Edinburgh: T. & T. Clark, 1906), 1: 9.

7. John Gardner, *On Moral Fiction* (New York: Basic Books, Inc., 1978), 67.
8. "I see," she said at last, thoughtfully, "I see now. This garden is like the Stable. It is far bigger inside than it was outside."

   "Of course, Daughter of Eve," said the Faun. "The farther up and the farther in you go, the bigger everything gets. The inside is larger than the outside." (C. S. Lewis, *The Last Battle* [Middlesex, England: Penguin Books, 1967], 162.
9. Hans Urs von Balthasar, *The Glory of the Lord* (San Francisco: Ignatius Press, 1982), 1: 218.

Chapter 3: Language

Epigraph: Eugen Rosenstock-Huessy, *Speech and Reality* (Norwich, VT: Argo Books, Inc., 1970), 145.
1. Bernard Lonergan provides the twentieth century equivalent of Thomas. His careful and relentless exposition of the whole person as an instrument of both mind and spirit in all matters of learning and growth, but above all in matters theological, reinvolves every person who prays in all the disciplines of the way of prayer. See especially his *Method in Theology* (New York: Seabury Press, 1972).
2. Max Black, *The Importance of Language* (Ithaca, NY: Cornell University Press, 1962), Foreword, no page number.
3. Eugene H. Peterson, "First Language," *Theology Today* 42 (July 1985): 211.
4. Walter Wangerin, Jr., *The Orphean Passages* (San Francisco: Harper & Row, 1986), 48. He also gives an extended reflection on how the three forms of language are kept healthy in a living faith. See especially p. 54–61.
5. "That true prayer lives in religions testifies to their true life; as long as it lives in them, they live. Degeneration of religions means the degeneration of prayer in them: the relational power in them is buried more and more by objecthood; they find it ever more difficult to say You with their whole undivided being." (Martin Buber, *I and Thou*, trans. Walter Kaufmann (New York: Charles Scribner's Sons, 1970), 167.
7. Karl Barth, *Anselm: Fides Quaerens Intellectum*, trans. Ian W. Robertson, (New York: Meridian Books, The World Publishing Co., 1962), 36.

Chapter 4: Story

Epigraph: Reynolds Price, *A Palpable God* (San Francisco: North Point Press, 1985), 14.
1. Brevard Childs, *Introduction to the Old Testament as Scripture* (Philadelphia: Fortress Press, 1979), 520.
2. Peter Ackroyd, *Doors of Perception: A Guide to Reading the Psalms* (London: SCM Press, 1978), 35–36, 74–76.
3. Annie Dillard, *Teaching a Stone to Talk* (New York: Harper & Row, 1982), 55.
4. I am paraphrasing and adapting Martin Buber. His words are: "He, to whom and by whom the word is spoken, is in the full sense of the word a person. Before the word is spoken by him in human language it is spoken to him in another language, from which he has to translate it into human language, to him this word is spoken as between person and person. In order to speak to

man, God must become a person; but in order to speak to him He must make him too a person. . . . Only Jeremiah of all the Israelite prophets has dared to note this bold and devout life conversation of the utterly inferior with the utterly superior—in such a measure is man here become a person. All Israelite relationship of faith is dialogic; here the dialogue has reached its pure form. Man can speak, he is permitted to speak; if only he truly speaks to God, there is nothing he may not say to him." (Martin Buber, *The Prophetic Faith*, (New York: The MacMillan Co., 1949], 164–65.)

Chapter 5: Rhythm

Epigraph: Odysseas Elytis, *"First Things First,"* trans. Olga Broumas, *American Poetry Review 17*, (January/February 1988); 10.

1. From a 1961 lecture in New York City. No language is better equipped to "shake" than the Hebrew language. The rhythms are strong, throbbing, and usually regular. Words are short. Sentences are simple. The sound system and syntax combine to produce heavily rhythmic speech. By its basic nature, Hebrew is incapable of Greek and Latin subtleties of rhythmic variation. The syntax prohibits iambic pentameters; the phonology makes a dactyl next to impossible. "Most of us have stood upon the beach in heavy weather, and have watched the waves driven by the wind upon the shore. As far as sight can reach there is a mass of hurrying crests, and the eye picks out and follows one of these in its rapid progress till it is caught by the shelving sand and curls to break. Then there is a pause, as it were, a moment of fancied suspense, before the water falls. I never see this sight without thinking of a Hebrew word or thought-phrase, and never have this picture far in the background of my mind as I read Hebrew for myself. You have from the start that same hurrying movement, almost impatient of the obstacles presented by the intractable pure long vowels, surmounting such as may lie in its way, and speeding eagerly till it nears the tone, and then the whole hangs for a moment in suspense in the immediate pretone, before it falls with all its crashing force of sound and sense upon the great word-accent. So powerful is this ictus that it supersedes all other laws of rhythm natural to the Hebrew language, and gives dispensation for such monstrosities as a short vowel in an open syllable and a long vowel in a closed syllable." (T. H. Robinson, *The Genius of Hebrew Grammar* [London: Humphrey Milford, 1928], 8.

2. James Muilenburg in his introduction to H. Gunkel, *The Psalms, A Form-Critical Introduction* (Philadelphia: Fortress Press, 1967), iv.

3. Dante Alighieri, *The Divine Comedy: Paradise*, trans. Dorothy Sayers and Barbara Reynolds (Baltimore: Penguin Books, 1962), 347.

4. I don't like the man who doesn't sleep, says God.
   Sleep is the friend of man.
   Sleep is the friend of God.
   Sleep is perhaps the most beautiful thing I have created,
      and I myself rested on the seventh day.
   He whose heart is pure, sleeps, And he who sleeps has a pure heart.
   That is the great secret of being as indefatigable as a child,
      of having that strength in legs that a child has.

Those new legs, those new souls,
And to begin afresh every morning, ever new,
Like young hope, new hope.
But they tell me that there are men
Who work well and sleep badly.
Who don't sleep. What a lack of confidence in me.

I pity them. I have it against them. A little, they don't trust me.
Like the child who innocently lies in his mother's arms, thus they do
    not lie
Innocently in the arm of my Providence.
They have the courage to work. They haven't enough virtue to be idle.
To stretch out. To rest. To sleep.
Poor people, they don't know what is good.
They look after their business very well during the day.
But they haven't enough confidence in me to let me look after it
    during the night.
As if I wasn't capable of looking after it during one night.
He who doesn't sleep is unfaithful to Hope.
And it is the greatest infidelity."
(Charles Peguy, *Basic Verities* [New York: Pantheon Books, 1943], 209–11.

5. Francis de Sales, *Introduction to the Devout Life*, trans. John K. Ryan (Garden City, NY: Image Books, Doubleday & Co., Inc., 1955), 157–63.
6. Quoted in Maisie Ward, *Gilbert Keith Chesterton* (Baltimore: Penguin Books, 1958), 397.
9. Karl Barth, *Church Dogmatics* (Edinburgh: T. and T. Clark, 1962), III/4, p. 107.

Chapter 6: Metaphor

Epigraph: Quoted by Joe Tharpe, in *Walker Percy* (Boston: Twayne Publishing Co., 1983), 13.
1. John Calvin, *Institutes of the Christian Religion* (Philadelphia: Westminster Press, 1960), 72, 171, 61, 341, and frequently in his commentaries.
2. Annie Dillard, *Pilgrim at Tinker Creek* (New York: Harper & Row, 1974), 233.
3. Virginia Stem Owens, *And the Trees Clap their Hands* (Grand Rapids, MI: William B. Eerdmans Publishing Co., 1983), 16. The book is a brilliant diagnosis and antidote to this pervasive spiritual sickness. Another comprehensive treatment, with concentrated attention on its North American forms, is Philip J. Lee, *Against the Protestant Gnostics* (New York: Oxford University Press, 1987).
4. C. S. Lewis, *Mere Christianity* (New York: The MacMillan Co., 1976), 65.
5. See especially, Baron Friedrich von Hügel, *Essays and Addresses on the Philosophy of Religion*, second series (London: J. M. Dent and Sons, 1926).

Chapter 7: Liturgy

Epigraph: Cynthia Ozick, *The Cannibal Galaxy* (New York: Alfred A. Knopf, 1983), 88–89.
1. Jerome, in his letter to Marcella, favors the first explanation; he compares

the use of the word with that of *Amen* or *Shalom* to mark the end of a passage and confirm its contents, a pause in which a benediction can be inserted. Most modern scholars agree. The Septuagint translation, "interlude" *(diapsalma),* is consistent with this. A few, Ewald notably, argue that it means "loud." One scholar conjectures that it is a signal that cymbals should interrupt the even flow of chant. See Charles A. Briggs, *A Critical and Exegetical Commentary the Book of Psalms* (Edinburgh: T. & T. Clark, 1906), 1: lxxxvii, and *Interpreters Dictionary of the Bible,* 3: 460.

Lacking a clear consensus from the scholars I have felt free to offer the less scholarly but more entertaining suggestion that *Selah* is a Philistine expletive that David learned during those hard years when he was banished from Saul's court and knocking around with ruffians and outlaws in the wilderness. He used it whenever he broke a string on his harp.

2. Sigmund Mowinckel demolished the wildly mistaken scholarly assumption that interpreted the Psalms almost exclusively as the expression of private religion. The interpreters, he wrote, "more or less consciously all shared that contempt of ordered ecclesiastical worship which was common to pietism, revivalist movements, rationalism, and liberalism. Often coming from pietistically influenced circles themselves, they took it for granted that such groups had existed in Judaism as well, and found there the birthplace of psalmody." (Sigmund Mowinckel, *The Psalms in Israel's Worship,* trans. D. R. Ap-Thomas [Oxford: Basil Blackwell, 1962], 1: 13.)

3. Helmer Ringgren, *The Faith of the Psalmists* (Philadelphia: Fortress Press, 1963), 1.

4. "The liturgists have largely had themselves to thank for the reverent disregard with which their labours are so generally treated. They persist in presenting their subject as a highly specialized branch of archaeology with chiefly aesthetic preoccupations, as though the liturgy had evolved of itself in a sort of ecclesiastical vacuum remote from the real life and needs of men and women, who have always had to lead their spiritual lives while helping to carry on the whole muddled history of a redeemed yet fallen world. Archaeology is no doubt fascinating to specialists but it is a recondite business. And though beauty is an attribute to God and as such can be fittingly employed in His worship, it is only a means to that end and in most respects not a directly necessary means. The ordinary man knows very well that prayer and communion with God have their difficulties, but that these arise less from their own technique than from the nature of human life. Worship is a mysterious but also a very direct and commonplace human activity. It is meant for the plain man to do, to whom it is an intimate and sacred but none the less quite workaday affair. He therefore rightly refuses to pray on strictly archaeological principles." (Dom Gregory Dix, *The Shape of the Liturgy* [London: Dacre Press, 1945], xiv.)

5. *The Collected Works of St. John of the Cross,* trans. Kieran Kavanaugh, O.C.D. and Otilio Rodriguez, O.C.D. (Washington, DC: Institute of Carmelite Studies, 1979), 122, 228.

6. "The crucial historical critical discovery of this came with the form-critical work of H. Gunkel who established conclusively that the historical settings of the psalms were not to be sought in particular historical events, but in the

cultic life of the community." (Brevard Childs, *Introduction to the Old Testament as Scripture* [Philadelphia: Fortress Press, 1979], 509.

Chapter 8: Enemies

Epigraph: Ernest Becker, *The Denial of Death* (New York: The Free Press, 1973), 283.

1. "The victim who speaks in the Psalms seems not in the least 'moral,' not evangelic enough for the good apostles of modern times. The sensibilities of our humanists are shocked. Usually, the unfortunate victim turns to hate those who hate him. The display of violence and resentment 'so characteristic of the Old Testament' is deplored, and is seen as a particularly clear indication of the famous malice of the God of Israel. Ever since Neitzsche people have seen in the Psalms the invention of all the bad feeling infecting us, humiliation, and resentment. We are offered in contrast to the venomous Psalms the beautiful serenity of mythologies, particularly Greek and German. Strong in their righteousness, and convinced that their victim is truly guilty, persecutors have no reason to be troubled.

"The victim of the Psalms is disturbing, it is true, and even annoying compared with an Oedipus who has the good taste to join in the wonderful classic harmony. See with what art and delicacy, at the given moment, he denounces himself. He brings to it the enthusiasm of the psychoanalytic patient on the couch or the old Bolshevist in the time of Stalin. Make no mistake, he provides a model for the supreme conformism of our time which is no different from the blustering of avant-gardism. Our intellectuals are so eager for servitude that they formed their Stalinist cells before Stalinism was invented. How can we be surprised that they have waited fifty years or more before making discreet inquiries into the greatest persecutions in human history. Mythology is the very best school in the training of silence. We never hesitate between the Bible and mythology. We are classicists first, romantics second, and primitives when necessary, modernists with a fury, neoprimitives when we are disgusted with modernism, gnostics always, but biblical never." (Rene Girard, *The Scapegoat* [Baltimore: Johns Hopkins University Press, 1987], 104.

3. Walter Klise, *The Last Western* (Allen, TX: Argus Communications, 1974), 126.

4. Walter Brueggemann, *The Message of the Psalms* (Minneapolis: Augsburg Publishing House, 1984), 77.

5. The "cruelest verb" is *edaphidzo* (Luke 19:44), "dash [your babies] to the ground." This is its only occurrence in the New Testament.

6. See Dietrich Bonhoeffer, *The Psalms: The Prayer Book of the Bible*, trans. James H. Burtness (Minneapolis: Augsburg Publishing House, 1974).

Chapter 9: Memory

Epigraph: Czeslaw Milosz in his 1980 Nobel Lecture, quoted in *The New York Review of Books*, 5 May 1981, p. 12.

1. The image is from Walter Hilton: "they strive and fight all day against sins

and for the getting of virtues; and sometimes they are above and sometime beneath, as wrestlers are." (*The Scale of Perfections*, ed. Evelyn Underhill [London: Watkins, 1948], part II, section 36.)

2. "Pied Beauty," in *Gerard Manley Hopkins: A Selection of His Poems and Prose*, ed. W. H. Gardner (Baltimore: Penguin Books, 1953), 30.

3. The phrase is by Frederick Buechner, *The Alphabet of Grace* (New York: The Seabury Press, 1977), 37.

4. Will Bradbury, quoted by William Zinsser, *On Writing Well* (New York: Harper & Row, 1985), 138.

5. The title of the book of culture criticism by novelist Walker Percy (New York: Farrar, Straus and Giroux, 1983).

6. Eudora Welty, *One Writer's Beginning*, (Cambridge, MA: Harvard University, 1984), 90.

7. "Lead Kindly Light," *The Hymnbook* (Philadelphia: Presbyterian Church, 1955), 281.

8. Referred to by Frank Kermode, *The Sense of an Ending* (New York: Oxford University Press, 1967), 52.

Chapter 10: End

Epigraph: T. S. Eliot, "Little Gidding," in *The Complete Poems and Plays 1909–1950* (New York: Harcourt Brace and Co., 1958), 144.

1. H. Gunkel and J. Begrich, *Einleitung in die Psalmen* (Göttingen, 1933), 173.

2. B. A. G. Fuller, *History of Philosophy* (New York: Henry Holt & Co., 1945), 178–79.

3. José Ortega y Gasset, *What is Philosophy?* (New York: W. W. Norton & Co., 1960), 243.

4. "One of the striking features of the Psalter in its canonical form is the large number of psalms which sound dominant eschatological notes. 'I wait for Yahweh more than the watchman for the morning' (130.5). 'Yahweh will build Zion, he will appear in his glory' (102.15). Cf. Pss. 69.34; 126.4ff.

"However one explains it , the final form of the Psalter is highly eschatological in nature. It looks forward to the future and passionately yearns for its arrival. Even when the psalmist turns briefly to reflect on the past in praise of the 'great things which Yahweh has done,' invariably the movement shifts and again the hope of salvation is projected into the future (126.6). The perspective of Israel's worship in the Psalter is eschatologically oriented." (Brevard Childs, *Introduction to the Old Testament as Scripture* [Philadelphia: Fortress Press, 1979], 517–18.)

5. Karl Barth, *Church Dogmatics* (Edinburgh: T. And T. Clark, 1961), III/4, p. 377. Also: " 'I rejoice' usually means—there is nothing wrong in this—'I rejoice in anticipation.' Most joy is anticipatory. Even in the experience of the fulfillment, and particularly when this experience is genuine, it usually changes immediately into anticipatory joy, i.e., joy in expectation of further fulfillment. In this respect, it normally has something of an eschatological character."

6. The most dramatic pivot in the Psalms is at 22:22.

7. *The Collected Works of St. Teresa of Avila*, trans. Kieran Kavanaugh, O.C.D. and

Otilio Rodriguez, O.C.D. (Washington, DC: Institute of Carmelite Studies, 1976), 2:246.

8. In the Hebrew text the N (nun) is omitted, leaving only twenty-one letters. It probably dropped out accidentally in transmission since the Greek translation (the Septuagint) has it.

9. See Harvey H. Guthrie, Jr., *Theology as Thanksgiving: From Israel's Psalms to the Church's Eucharist* (New York: The Seabury Press, 1981).

10. Annie Dillard's conclusion to *Pilgrim at Tinker Creek*, her profoundly contemplative exegesis of the creation, having persistently pushed through much pain and enigma in the process, arrives at a similar and psalmic conclusion: "I think that the dying pray at the last not 'please' but 'thank you,' as a guest thanks his host at the door. Falling from airplanes the people are crying thank you, thank you, all down the air; and the cold carriages draw up for them on the rocks. Divinity is not playful. The universe was not made in jest but in solemn incomprehensible earnest. By a power that is unfathomably secret, and holy, and fleet. There is nothing to be done about it, but ignore it, or see. And like Billy Bray I go my way, and my left foot says 'Glory,' and my right foot says 'Amen' in and out of Shadow Creek, upstream and down, exultant, in a daze, dancing, to the twin silver trumpets of praise." (Annie Dillard, *Pilgrim at Tinker Creek* [New York: Harper's Magazine Press, 1974], 270–71.)

11. The Westminster Shorter Catechism begins where the Psalter ends. "Question 1: What is the chief end of man? Answer: To enjoy and glorify him forever."